R THE

PERSON

DIGNITY
REVOLUTION

STANDING UP FOR THE
VALUE OF EVERY PERSON

DIGNITY REVOLUTION
STANDING UP FOR THE VALUE OF EVERY PERSON

PUBLISHER
Life Promotions, Inc.
Appleton, Wisconsin

PROJECT DIRECTOR
Tammy Borden

GRAPHIC DESIGN
Hannah Ebb

ISBN 978-0-9856716-3-1

Library of Congress Catalog Number 2014939480

Printed in the United States of America

Life Promotions, Inc.
4 North Systems Drive, Suite C
Appleton, Wisconsin 54914
info@lifepromotions.com

Scripture taken from the *New American Standard Bible,*® copyright ©1995 The Lockman Foundation. Used by permission.

Proceeds (100%) from the sale of *Dignity Revolution* are designated for funding antibullying, suicide prevention, and value-based school assembly programs to promote the dignity of every person around the world.

Printed on 10% PCW sustainable source certified paper using soy-based inks.

FOR MY SISTER, LOIS.

Thank you. You are a huge part of my story as a person. You have taught me, and continue to teach me, so much about life. Most importantly, you have taught me that every person has value and that what matters most is love and how you treat people, things money can't buy.

You have shown me how love can change this world, and because of you, we will have a Dignity Revolution.

Love,
Your brother,

ACKNOWLEDGMENTS

FIRST OF ALL, I WANT TO THANK ALL OF THE STUDENTS WHO I HAVE SPOKEN TO FOR SO MANY YEARS.

YOU ARE AMAZING, AND YOU ARE WHY I DO WHAT I DO.

TO MY WIFE, CAROL, MY BEST FRIEND AND PARTNER IN EVERYTHING I DO.

TO THE STAFF OF LIFE PROMOTIONS FOR THEIR DEDICATION AND HARD WORK.

TO MARY ROCKMAN FOR THE EARLY YEARS, FORMING THE SELF-IMAGE BROCHURE AND THE CONCEPTS IN THIS BOOK.

TO MY DAUGHTER, AMBER, WHO TAUGHT ME SO MANY LESSONS AS WE WORKED TOGETHER ON THIS MANUSCRIPT. JUST BE YOU. YOU ROCK.

TO DEBORAH TACKMANN, WHOSE STRENGTHS FILLED IN THE "HOLES" OF THIS BOOK, THE MISSING PIECES OF THE PUZZLE, AND MADE THIS PROJECT A SUCCESS.

TO MY ASSISTANT, TAMMY BORDEN, WHO SO MANY PEOPLE KNOW IS LIKE A CO-AUTHOR OF THIS BOOK, FOR ALL THE THOUGHTS, IDEAS AND MANY HOURS OF TRYING TO READ MY WRITING, LISTENING TO MY DICTATION AND, AND, AND …

TO DEXTER, MY BROTHER FROM ANOTHER MOTHER, FOR TEAMING UP TO WRITE THE GROUP DISCUSSION QUESTIONS FOR THE BOOK. KEEP SPEAKING (*INFO@LIFEPROMOTIONS.COM*).

TO ARDAN JAMES, THE ANIMATED ILLUSIONIST,® WHO NOT ONLY HAS BEEN THE OPENING ACT FOR THOUSANDS OF SCHOOL AND COMMUNITY EVENTS, BUT IS PART OF OUR TEAM AND MY FRIEND (*INFO@LIFEPROMOTIONS.COM*).

TO JOHN DOUGHERTY, WHO "CARRIES STUFF" BETTER THAN ANYONE.

TO FAITH, AND FAMILY AND FRIENDS WHO MAKE IT ALL WORTHWHILE.

BOB LENZ

CONTENTS

CHAPTER 1

I DARE YOU

I've always wanted to stand up for the underdog, the person being put down, laughed at, harassed or bullied. An inner voice would say, "Speak up and rally others. Shout out, 'It's not right. They're a person, too. How would you feel if you were treated like that?'"

I really did want to make a difference. I even dreamed of it. But I caved to excuses—if I wasn't so insecure; if I was smarter or better looking; if I was stronger or a better speaker. Maybe if I was from a different family, or if I had lots of money to influence people, I would say every person matters, every person has dignity. Maybe then …

I had enough "ifs" in my life to convince me that I couldn't make a difference. I didn't like who I was. I wondered why my family had problems. I disliked allowing the opinions of others to dictate my choices and determine how I felt about myself. Deep inside I didn't care what other people looked like, how much money they had, what their title or position was, or what their external talents were. Still, I based my own value on those very same qualities, or lack of them. It brought me to the point of asking some tough questions: Does every person have a purpose? Does every life have value? Does mine?

If every life has value, why couldn't I be content with who I was? Why was I envious of others? There were so many times when I wished I was someone else. Why couldn't I have their life and make mine go away, like the time I didn't make the basketball team and all my friends did. I remember how I felt afterward, worthless, that I didn't measure up.

As insecure as I was, the truth is I was still arrogant in many ways. Though my mom always taught that we are all human beings, flaws and all, I sometimes saw myself as better than others. Because of that, I had some very humbling experiences. I continue to be challenged every day to see people for who they are deep inside, instead of judging their worth on what can only be seen on the outside.

And, I am still learning huge lessons, many of them from the very people I looked down upon at one time thinking I was the better person, those I wanted to stand up for and defend because I condescendingly thought they were "less" than me. But they are the ones who taught me, and continue to show me, that every person has worth and dignity, and how life is found in the intangibles. They've shown me what really matters most in life is not what we have, but who we are and how we treat others. We should be known as human beings, not "human doings."

I know life has disappointments, pain and problems, but why wouldn't we want to bring a smile and a helping hand to someone, anyone, if that's possible? Why would anyone want to cause more hurt and inflict more pain on those who are already feeling isolated and alone? Many would say that's cruel and downright evil. I'm sad to say I have done those very things, and the less I stood up for the lives of others, the less I felt alive. It's like Martin Luther King Jr. said, "Our lives begin to end the day we become silent about things that matter."

We don't have to be influenced or controlled by a society that tells us we're not good enough. We don't have to live as victims, falling into self-pity and despair over past experiences. Nor should we fight injustice with hatred. The answer lies elsewhere. We can become part of the solution. We can transform our world where lives have purpose and meaning for all, no matter what has been said or done to us, no matter our past mistakes, no matter what this life hands us. We can demonstrate resiliency when faced with life's challenges. Life is worth living.

I dare you. I dare you to become part of the Dignity Revolution, no matter what.

DOES EVERY PERSON HAVE A PURPOSE? DOES EVERY LIFE HAVE VALUE? DOES MINE?

DON'T BE FOOLED BY ME

Don't be fooled by me.
Don't be fooled by the face I wear
for I wear a mask, a thousand masks,
masks that I'm afraid to take off,
and none of them is me.

Pretending is an art that's second nature with me,
but don't be fooled,
for God's sake don't be fooled.
I give you the impression that I'm secure,
that all is sunny and unruffled with me, within as well as without,
that confidence is my name and coolness my game,
that the water's calm and I'm in command
and that I need no one,
but don't believe me.
My surface may seem smooth but my surface is my mask,
ever-varying and ever-concealing.
Beneath lies no complacence.
Beneath lies confusion, and fear, and aloneness.
But I hide this. I don't want anybody to know it.
I panic at the thought of my weakness exposed.
That's why I frantically create a mask to hide behind,
a nonchalant sophisticated facade,
to help me pretend,
to shield me from the glance that knows.
But such a glance is precisely my salvation, my only hope,
and I know it.
That is, if it's followed by acceptance,
if it's followed by love.
It's the only thing that can liberate me from myself,
from my own self-built prison walls,

from the barriers I so painstakingly erect.
It's the only thing that will assure me
of what I can't assure myself,
that I'm really worth something.
But I don't tell you this. I don't dare to, I'm afraid to.
I'm afraid your glance will not be followed by acceptance,
will not be followed by love.
I'm afraid you'll think less of me,
that you'll laugh, and your laugh would kill me.
I'm afraid that deep-down I'm nothing
and that you will see this and reject me.

So I play my game, my desperate pretending game,
with a facade of assurance without
and a trembling child within.
So begins the glittering but empty parade of masks,
and my life becomes a front.
I idly chatter to you in the suave tones of surface talk.
I tell you everything that's really nothing,
and nothing of what's everything,
of what's crying within me.
So when I'm going through my routine
do not be fooled by what I'm saying.
Please listen carefully and try to hear what I'm not saying,
what I'd like to be able to say,
what for survival I need to say,
but what I can't say.

I don't like hiding.
I don't like playing superficial phony games.
I want to stop playing them.

I want to be genuine and spontaneous and me
but you've got to help me.
You've got to hold out your hand
even when that's the last thing I seem to want.
Only you can wipe away from my eyes
the blank stare of the breathing dead.
Only you can call me into aliveness.
Each time you're kind, and gentle, and encouraging,
each time you try to understand because you really care,
my heart begins to grow wings—
very small wings,
very feeble wings,
but wings!

With your power to touch me into feeling
you can breathe life into me.
I want you to know that.
I want you to know how important you are to me,
how you can be a creator—an honest-to-God creator—
of the person that is me
if you choose to.
You alone can break down the wall behind which I tremble,
you alone can remove my mask,
you alone can release me from my shadow-world of panic,
from my lonely prison,
if you choose to.
Please choose to.

Do not pass me by.
It will not be easy for you.
A long conviction of worthlessness builds strong walls.
The nearer you approach to me
the blinder I may strike back.
It's irrational, but despite what the books say about man
often I am irrational.
I fight against the very thing I cry out for.
But I am told that love is stronger than strong walls
and in this lies my hope.
Please try to beat down those walls
with firm hands but with gentle hands
for a child is very sensitive.

Who am I, you may wonder?
I am someone you know very well.
For I am every man you meet
and I am every woman you meet.

"Please Hear What I'm Not Saying," *Charles C. Finn*[1]

Do you wish you could go to everyone for whom this poem is written and cry out, "I care. I want to say the words you've been longing to hear. I want to be the one who breathes life into you again. Don't give up. Don't give in to hopelessness. Please, let me show you what real love looks like."

Are you like me, realizing you need someone to speak these words to you, too? As I look at my life, there are people who have. There have been times when my masks have pushed people away. Yet, there were also times when their love slipped through and went straight to my heart.

For this to really be a book about emphasizing dignity and opposing bullying, we need to know how to build strength and resiliency, which empowers us to strip away our masks and break down walls. Life is going to have challenges, unexpected heartaches and difficulties. We need to allow people to be there for us during these times, and we need to be there for others. Most importantly, we need to choose hope and love over despair and contempt.

It will take more than good intentions to convince people of their value, to assure them that they needn't hide who they really are to feel accepted and loved. It's going to take a movement to reverse a system forged in our society that has convinced millions of people that who they are is not enough. It's going to take positive action and a commitment that begins with you and me today.

To truly have a Dignity Revolution, a "mask-free" society must be created where everyone has the innate right to feel valued and respected. We call this *dignity*, a state or quality of being worthy of honor and respect. We need to turn what is wrong into that which is right. This is called *revolution*, a fundamental change in thinking or society. It will take more than good intentions. Let's empower ourselves with the knowledge and skills it will take to begin this Dignity Revolution.

CHAPTER 3

YOU HAVE VALUE

Traveling the world and speaking in schools is one of my favorite things to do. Often, when I'm speaking in front of an entire school audience, I try to break the ice by approaching a student and asking, "Will you please stand and share your most embarrassing moment?"

Imagine you are that person. You're in a gymnasium among hundreds of your peers. Your heart races. Simultaneously, you experience a hot flash and break into a cold sweat. Your face turns red. Your mind goes blank. All this happens in a fraction of a second.

Then I assure the student that they don't have to speak. Instead, I share one of my most embarrassing moments. It happened when I was a senior in high school attending the prom, the last big dance, and my friends and I wanted to go out in style.

Nine of my friends and I rented the same tuxedo—well, technically not the same one, but they all looked identical. In the town where I'm from, there is a tradition. We attend church before going to prom. There we all sat, in the front pew with our dates. Because of our match-ing tuxedos, the priest thought we were the prom court, so he asked if we would like to march out together at the close of the service. We said, "Sure, why not?" So, there we were, marching out in our match-ing tuxes, our dates on our arms. Everyone thought we were the prom court—except, of course, the prom court.

When I was in high school, John Travolta was popular—the *first* time. It wasn't because of movies like *Pulp Fiction, Get Shorty* or *Wild Hogs*. Rather, it was for a film called *Saturday Night Fever* and another called *Grease*. It was the era of disco dancing, which played a signifi-cant role in my story.

Soon after we arrived at the prom we headed for the dance floor. There we were, trying our best to imitate John Travolta, pointing to the ceiling, then to the floor in rhythm to the music, with an occasional ex-aggerated swing of the hips. As we danced, a wall of people slowly gath-ered around us. I'm not sure if it was because of their admiration for our great dancing, or their concern that we might injure ourselves with our crazy moves. Nevertheless, they began shouting, "More, more!"

...IF WE WAIT UNTIL WE HAVE EVERTHING SOCIETY IMPLIES WE NEED BEFORE WE DO WHAT'S RIGHT, THEN WE'LL NEVER BE PART OF A DIGNITY REVOLUTION.

Besides pointing to the ceiling and floor, I tried to recall what more John Travolta had done in the films. Then I remembered. It was one of his signature moves. He leaped high into the air and came down doing the splits. Before I knew it, I was caught up in the moment and found myself leaping into the air. On my way down, for a split second I thought *this will really impress the girls*. My legs hit bottom, splayed outward against the wooden planks of the gym floor. Then I heard it: *r-r-r-i-p*.

My pants tore from the belt loop down to the knee. Now, this wasn't just any small tear. It was monumental. It was ventilation—big time! This would have been no big deal had dancers been scattered around the room, no one to notice if I just turned and ran. But about 50 of my classmates surrounded me. No matter which way I turned, there was someone pointing and laughing.

Since then, I've learned that I am not the only one who has had an embarrassing moment or two. I've heard hundreds of other stories of outrageous and embarrassing moments that could make you laugh for hours.

On the flip side, others have experienced embarrassing moments whose stories are not funny at all. Many students have said, "For me, it's not an embarrassing moment. I'm embarrassed about who I am as a person." For them, an embarrassing situation became a humiliating experience. Those moments of humiliation triggered a question about their identity and dignity.

What is it that makes the difference? Why are some people able to walk away from a public mishap and simply think *that was embarrassing*? Yet, others are ashamed and think in their heart *I'm a nobody*. It's the element of choice. I believe the difference comes when someone chooses to humiliate another person.

Most of us have embarrassing moments. Imagine you're walking down the hall at school and stumble, and your books go flying. What would you do? First, you'd brace your fall and look around to see if anyone saw you. If so, you'd nervously grin, chuckle, wave, pick up your books and think *duh!* Later, you'd probably laugh while telling your friends about your embarrassing moment.

Now consider the opposite of that situation. You fall, your books go flying, and you look around to see who was looking. This time, there is a group of people staring, laughing and pointing, one of them with a foot extended. You realize your fall was intentional. You were purposely tripped in an effort to belittle you and strip you of your dignity.

When someone makes a conscious choice to hurt, humiliate, harass, make fun of, degrade, put down, or bully another human being, the individual who has been targeted becomes a victim and may begin to question their identity. When we are humiliated by another person, we have likely become a steppingstone for that person's own fragile identity.

I'm not proud to admit it, but I can remember stepping on other people to build myself up. In my school, if you were a guy of any size, you played football. If you were big and didn't play football, some would label you and call you names. For them, it wasn't okay to pursue your own talents or dreams. It wasn't acceptable to just be *you*. That's the way it was.

I was a starting player on the team; I felt good about that. There was another guy on our team whose name was Jack. It still is. He wasn't very good at football. I'm not putting him down. It was just not where his natural gifts or talents lay. Jack wanted to be a part of the team so badly. He came to practice early every day and stayed late just to fit in, just to belong.

The truth is Jack made the team only because the coach never cut anyone. Did the "starters" accept him as part of the team? I wish I could say yes, but the reality is no. He was laughed at, mocked and used as a blocking dummy, all at his expense.

One day after practice, as I hung out in the middle of the field, someone called out, "Look at Jack." I turned and saw how other starters had grabbed Jack and hung him on a fence post by his jersey. I'm ashamed to admit it, but I laughed along with everyone else. There hung Jack, arms and legs dangling and flailing as he tried to get down.

I enjoyed the prank; that is, until I walked by Jack on the way to the locker room. I saw how humiliated he was. What gripped my heart most were the tears streaming down his face. I hung my head in shame as I walked by and thought *Jack didn't deserve that. He never did anything to hurt our team. He actually would have done anything to help the team. He just wanted to belong. He just wanted to fit in.*

Experts have told me that the number one reason people join gangs is for a sense of belonging. What really makes me sad is that some gangs would have treated Jack better than our team and school treated him.

After sharing this story at a high school, the captain of the football team approached me and said, "That's a powerful story, but you have to finish it." I asked him what he meant, and he said, "You need to tell everyone how you helped Jack down from the fence and became his friend."

I'm sorry to say I couldn't do that, and still can't, because all my stories are true. I knew what had been done to Jack was wrong, but I didn't help. I didn't stand up for him. I was as guilty as my fellow teammates who hung Jack on the fence because I did nothing. So, why didn't I do what was right? Why didn't I speak up for Jack? Because these were the guys I wanted to be "in" with, too.

This book is not written to tell you what you should or shouldn't do. You need to do what you believe is right. I believe that is written on your heart. But I have found this to be true—the right choice isn't always the popular choice, and the popular choice isn't always the right one.

. . . THE RIGHT CHOICE ISN'T ALWAYS THE POPULAR CHOICE, THE POPULAR CHOICE ISN'T ALWAYS THE RIGHT ONE.

I chose what was popular because I didn't like who I was. Truth be told, I always wanted to be like my friend, Ronny. He was good-looking. When Ronny walked into a room, the girls would flirt with him, wave and sheepishly say, "Hi, Ronny." When I walked into a room, the girls would ask if I could arrange dates for them with Ronny. He was also athletic. He could take two steps and do a flip. I can take 100 steps and still can't do a flip. Ronny could jump off the "high dive" and do whatever he wanted with his body. I jump off the "high dive" and "splat"; the water does whatever it wants with my body.

Not only was Ronny good-looking and athletic, but he was the kind of guy who came by good grades easily. I did really well in school, too—except for grades. Even when I did my best and took books home to study, or studied in study hall (now there's a concept!), the best I earned was a *B*. Now, there's nothing wrong with a *B*, but Ronny aced everything, even when he didn't study. I don't ever recall that he carried a book home. And to top it off, Ronny's parents had money.

Can you relate to this? Have you ever thought *it's not fair? Why does this person have good looks, athletic talent, intelligence and money?*

If I possessed just one of Ronny's qualities, I thought, well, then maybe I could have stood up for what was right, helped Jack down from the fence and could have become his friend. But if we wait until we have everything society implies we need before we do what's right, then we'll never be part of a Dignity Revolution. Even if we have everything society says we need to be happy, be assured that, without good choices, a great life is not guaranteed.

I found this out one night when I arrived home to find my brother, Bill, waiting up for me. I knew something was wrong. When I asked him what was up, nothing could have prepared me for what I heard next. Ronny was dead.

I'll never forget the words and the emotion and confusion that raced through my mind. When I asked how it happened I was only more baffled when I was told that Ronny got drunk and had taken his life. How could it be? Ronny had it all, everything anyone could ask for. To this day, I can't find words that will take away the past, or take away your pain or problems, but you don't have to let your problems, pain or the past take away your choices. You still have a choice.

Ronny considered me one of his best friends and, because of that, his parents asked me to speak at his funeral. His body wasn't to be viewed at the funeral, so his family asked me to join them in paying respects at the funeral home. I'll never forget walking in with Ronny's mom and dad on one side and Ronny's girlfriend on the other. We stood there in tragic silence as Ronny came into the room, not with two steps and a flip, but on a cold, metal cart in a blue body bag. There laid my friend, never to laugh again, never to dance again, never again to do a flip, go to a concert or play racquetball, never again to have a friend by his side during the hard times … lifeless.

Questions raced through my mind. Why? How could Ronny not know he was valuable? How could he throw his life away? He was good-looking, athletic, intelligent and his parents had money. If he didn't feel significant, how could I? If he couldn't find purpose in life, what hope was there for Bob?

There are lots of reasons why people have problems and struggle with depression and suicidal thoughts. They range from chemical imbalances to not knowing how to cope with life's circumstances in a healthy way. Whether suffering abuse or being "labeled" with a diagnosis—chemical imbalance, attention deficit hyperactivity disorder, depression, bipolar disorder or some other condition—it's important to understand you are not "less" than others. Don't let your label limit you. Don't feel ashamed or convinced that you are not worthy of dignity, love and life. Don't be afraid to ask for help.

Though I didn't know the extent of his pain, some of my endless questions about Ronny were answered when his mom began unloading her guilt to me. She gave me a glimpse of what Ronny's life was like behind closed doors, a life I never knew.

If Ronny did something wrong when he was young, his mother would hit him, not spank or discipline him, but hit him. No one deserves that, *no one*.

When he was three, Ronny spilled some milk like all kids have done. His mom went to backhand him across the face, but because he had been hit before, Ronny instinctively raised his tiny arm to protect himself. The back of her hand hit his elbow instead. She told me of her annoyance and anger as the physical pain stung her hand. She lost it, and started hitting and kicking her three-year-old son. She threw him against a wall. When she finally tamed her anger, Ronny's little body was so badly bruised and bloody, his mother said, that she had to keep him in the house for more than a month so no one would see him and report it to officials.

When he was seven, there were problems in the neighborhood. When the police came, Ronny stood by his two sisters. "Are these your children?" the officer asked his mom. "These are my two girls," she said, referencing her daughters. Pointing to Ronny, she told the officer, "I don't know who that wild animal belongs to."

When Ronny was 13 he started to fight back. "I went to hit him and he grabbed my arm," his mother told me. Ronny looked her in the face sternly and said, "Mom, no more." She swung her other fist at him. He grabbed that one also, and told his mother to stop. She lost her temper yet again, violently screaming and struggling to gain control. She pulled his arm toward her and, in her rage, clenched Ronny's wrist in her teeth, sinking to the bone. Yes, Ronny required stitches because his mother bit him.

I wish Ronny's story was a fictional example used for shock value and to make a point but, sadly, it's true.

Tears flowed as Ronny's mom confessed to the abuse of her son. If these were the stories she was willing to share, it was difficult to imagine how awful it had really been for my friend.

Ronny never talked about any of the abuses. They were family secrets. So many of us believe our family is the only family with problems. No one else appears to struggle. No other family seems to fight like our

IF YOU, OR SOMEONE YOU KNOW, ARE THE TARGET OF ANY TYPE OF ABUSE, BREAK THE SILENCE. TELL SOMEONE, ANYONE . . .

own. Fill in the blank for the defenses you put up, and the excuses given for not sharing with others what happens in your family. Maybe that was Ronny's problem—he pushed away the pain and hid behind masks and walls until it wasn't tolerable anymore.

Ronny's mom needed help. Unfortunately, she didn't seek or receive the support she so desperately needed. Instead, she treated her son like garbage without respect or dignity. Over time, Ronny started believing it was true, that he was worthless and unworthy of love or life. He believed he was just trash.

Even after learning how horrible Ronny's home life must have been, I don't understand his taking his life. There were so many other options. He isn't the only person who has come from a dysfunctional, broken or imperfect family. If yours is a loving family, one that you know cares about you, thank them. Give them a hug. Tell them that you love them and that you are grateful for how they have cared for you. Really, do it! Oh, they might freak out. Because it's so out of the ordinary, they may even ask, "What's up? Are you going to ask for mon-

ey again?" For anyone in your life who has shown how valued you are as a person—teacher, coach, mentor, aunt or uncle—thank them, too.

If you feel like no one cares, I want to show you how no one can strip away your value, that you have value and dignity despite what may have happened to you.

If I took a five-dollar bill from you and asked, "How much is this worth?" you'd say, "Five dollars, of course."

What if I verbally abuse it and tell it, "You good-for-nothing five-dollar bill. I wish you had never been printed. You'll never be as good as your brother, the ten-dollar bill."

Now how much is it worth? Five dollars. Even though it has been verbally abused, it has not lost its value.

What if I physically abuse it? "Take that, Lincoln. You call that a beard? You can smile now. The war is over."

It's still five dollars. Okay, how about if I crumple it? Then I throw it on the floor, step on it and ask again, "How much is your money worth?"

Five dollars.

Now it's been physically abused, but it still hasn't lost its value. What if I spit on it? You may not want to touch it afterward, but it still has value.

What if the parents of the five-dollar bill get divorced and it becomes a forgotten five-dollar bill? What if its government shuts down and it spends all its time at home, lonely and neglected? Not even PlayStation 3 will play with it. What if everyone around it rejects it?

If it was not wanted by anyone, would it lose its value? No. Change its value? No.

If, after all this, I offered the five-dollar bill to someone else, do you think they would say, "No thanks, I don't want it. It's been laughed at, abused and neglected. Get it away from me." Of course not.

However, when those same things happen to us, we begin to think there is something wrong with us. We doubt our value as our dignity is stripped away.

If I took your five-dollar bill and tore it into pieces, how much is it worth? Five dollars.

Would you throw it away? No. Why? Because it still has value. It's still worth something.

I actually did this once and tried taping all the pieces back together. I was concerned when I discovered a piece was missing. When I nervously handed the "incomplete" bill to the teller at the bank, she handed over a brand new five-dollar bill in exchange without hesitation. She told me as long as it had the identification number it hadn't lost its value.

When we are abused or bullied with words or actions, or make mistakes in our lives, we doubt our self-worth. Almost every target of abuse, at some point, believes it is somehow their fault. It's staggering how many people think they're to blame, believe there is something wrong with them, or that they somehow deserved the abuse. Many times they throw their lives away to drugs, alcohol and other destructive choices, and end up in the landfill of regret. Worse yet, many throw their lives away altogether like my friend, Ronny.

You have to remember that you are more than an identification number. You are a human being with a unique identity. We are all persons of value.

The damaged five-dollar bill had value because it had a government inscription, a number and a seal, its value verified. Believe me when I say your worth is so much more than that of a five-dollar bill. You have rights, dignity and value that can never be taken away, no matter what others have done to you.

In the United States, our basic freedoms give us value: the right to live, to be free of shame inflicted by others, and to pursue joy. The Bill of Rights of the U.S. Constitution confirms our value, addressing human dignity, human equality and liberty; and in the Pledge of Allegiance we hear "liberty and justice for *all*," not just the male, white, rich, athletic, attractive or intelligent, but *all*. Further, The U.S. Declaration of Independence declares: "We hold these truths to be self-evident, that all men [people] are created equal, that they are endowed by their Creator with certain unalienable Rights, that among these are Life, Liberty, and the pursuit of Happiness."

If you take away nothing else from this book, please know this: No matter what people have done to you, no matter how you have been treated, no matter what has been said to you or what mistakes you have made, you have not lost your value.

If you, or someone you know, are the target of any type of abuse, break the silence. *Tell someone, anyone*—a parent, a friend, a counselor or law enforcement. If you are uncertain about what to do, call one of the national abuse hotlines below. Saying or doing nothing allows the abuse to continue.

National Domestic Abuse Hotline **800.799.SAFE** (800.799.7233)
National Child Abuse Hotline **800.4.A.CHILD** (800.422.4453)

CHAPTER 4

THE SYSTEM ISN'T WORKING

In the last chapter, I shared an embarrassing moment with you, but I saved this one for this chapter because it's one of my favorites. It was told to me at a speaking event in Santa Maria, California. You'll realize why it's easy for me to repeat it since it didn't happen to me personally.

A guy and a girl were on their first date. They decided to go to a movie. It was a decent movie, rated G: *Bambi* (part 3). It's a good flick! Can you imagine if the producers and creators of some of the horror flicks with Jason or Freddy got hold of a movie like *Bambi*? It would probably go something more like this: *Bambi* (part 3), *Bambi Kills Thumper*. By the way, make sure you pick out movies that are in line with your family's values.

Back to the story. This guy and girl made their way into the theater and found their seats. Now, I wish I knew why this happens, but when we guys get nervous, we need to use the rest room. Needless to say, this guy was pretty nervous, first date and all, so soon after sitting down he decided he needed to excuse himself. Wanting to be a gentleman, he …

Time out! I'd like to sidetrack here a little. Have you noticed that the word *gentleman* is disappearing today? In fact, the only place I seem to see the word is on rest room doors. There are a lot of people in society who will not stand up for what is right. There are a lot of "macho" guys who don't think it's manly to show an emotion, share a

hug, embrace, or shed a tear. We need kind, compassionate, sensitive, loving men who are gentle enough to be strong, yet strong and masculine enough to be gentle.

Every time I speak in a high school about the attributes of a true gentleman, there are girls in the audience who seem to respond, "Ooh, where is he?" Come on, guys, let's step it up and be "gentle men."

Now, continuing the story, trying his best to be a gentleman, the guy excused himself and made his way to the rest room.

When he returned, he sat down and, in a moment of panic, noticed his fly was open. He could feel the embarrassment building, blood rushing to his face. He wanted to hide, but had nowhere to go. He began to think of ways he could solve the problem without his friend noticing. Then, he had an idea. He would ask if she wanted popcorn and a soda. If and when she said yes, he would stand up, zip up and go for the snacks.

"Do you want popcorn and a soda?" he asked. "Sure," she replied. It was just what he hoped to hear and thought *this plan is working perfectly*. So he casually stood up, turned slightly and zipped up. *Smooth, real smooth*, he thought to himself. Feeling a huge sense of relief, he took a confident step toward the aisle. Suddenly, a deafening scream echoed throughout the entire theater. It came from a girl seated directly in front of him … who had really long hair.

. . . THE VAST MAJORITY OF HIGH SCHOOL STUDENTS . . . WILL CONFIDE IN A FRIEND BEFORE ANYONE ELSE.

You guessed it. Her hair was caught. What now? He couldn't simply undo it and say, "Oops, sorry." No, the zipper was stuck, really stuck.

The screaming continued and an usher came with a flashlight. After finding out what the commotion was all about, the usher tried to help but he couldn't free the girl's hair. As if that wasn't bad enough, the house lights came on and the movie was stopped in front of a packed audience. Having run out of options, the usher left for a moment and returned with a pair of scissors. With everyone watching, he freed the girl's hair.

The guy told me when it was all over, the entire theater stood up and gave him a standing ovation. The crowd of moviegoers had gotten more entertainment than they bargained for.

I can't imagine that kind of embarrassment.

After an unbelievable story like this one, I feel it's almost necessary to remind you that all my stories are true. In fact, you may be wondering how I came to hear them all.

I used to do peer facilitator workshops where students could learn how to help their friends and peers. We presented these workshops because the vast majority of high school students who struggle with a decision, problem, drugs, alcohol, sexuality or fears about their future, will confide in a friend before anyone else. As friends, we need to know how to listen and guide others to reliable resources that can really help them.

As part of the training, we formed a circle with about 10 people and asked everyone to share their most embarrassing moment. It was a blast. We laughed until our stomachs hurt.

Afterward, when most of the group had left the room, I would usually walk up to someone and ask, "Now that everyone's gone, is there another most embarrassing moment you haven't shared with the whole group?" Almost every single time, they nodded their head yes.

"Come on, tell. It has to be good if you don't want anyone to know." I would try to persuade them, telling them I would put it in my next book, but they still refused. "Why not?" I'd ask.

It's then that a tear usually trickled down their cheek. If there wasn't a tear—they had learned to hide their emotions behind walls and masks like you and I sometimes do—there was usually still a tear that came from their heart. If you have eyes trained through love to penetrate those kinds of masks, you'll see it. That's when a gentle heart of compassion springs into action to help the person explore what's really going on inside.

After years of talking with students, I've come to realize how many people struggle with their identity. To further explore how insecure someone is in their identity, I might ask, "If there was anything you could change about yourself, would you?" Nine out of 10 people respond, "Yes, if I could change something about me, I would."

There has to be a balance between the two extremes—people who are stuck-up, arrogant and think the whole world revolves around them, and people who don't think they have anything to offer society or their friends. Both are actually struggling to achieve a healthy identity.

As I study self-image, I've come to realize that even those who may look composed and stuck-up on the outside are oftentimes struggling on the inside with the same issues. They've just chosen a different mask. Some of the most arrogant, proud people I know can be the most insecure on the inside. Remember, sometimes the higher the wall on the outside, the deeper the pain on the inside.

When life screams out, "You don't matter, you're worthless, you're good for nothing," I feel the need to scream, "It's a LIE." I ask you to do the same, to combat what society says you have to be or have to do to feel good about yourself. I want you to stand up against society's system and join the Dignity Revolution for four reasons.

REASON 1

Society's system isn't working. If it's working, then why do nine out of 10 people say they would change something about themselves, and the tenth person probably should, too?

What would you change? I hesitate to write the responses I've received to that question, for they seem childish and almost cheesy, yet that's why I record them. I've felt these same insecurities at times and felt stupid, too. Those insecurities can easily paralyze a person inside and out.

One person told me he wanted to change his nose. I asked why and he told me how people called him Pinocchio all his life. Others told me they were called Porky Pig. Another person told me his chin was so long people thought it was a ski slope. Other examples include their voice, lack of musical ability or fear of speaking in public.

People always seem to want to change. Those who are short want to be taller; people who are tall wish they were shorter. People who have straight hair get it curled and those who have curly hair straighten it. People who have dark hair get it highlighted and people who have light hair get it tinted. People who have fair skin lie out all summer and get … cancer … uh, I mean tanned, and many people use tanning beds throughout the winter.

Americans spent almost $11 billion in 2012 on cosmetic procedures including breast implants, liposuction, facelifts, Botox, nose jobs, buttock lifts and a host of others.[1] These numbers rise incredibly each year. Despite all efforts, we're a nation filled with people still searching. Society's system for determining self-worth isn't working. I'm not saying no one should ever have corrective procedures. Yet, it's important to understand that the underlying motivation for many is because they're convinced they aren't acceptable the way they are.

I'm fair-skinned, so I try to stay out of the sun. You see, the sun is like a machine gun that splatters me with dots. They're called freckles. My mom would try to build my confidence when I was growing up by saying, "Bob, those aren't freckles. Those are angel kisses." I'd roll my eyes and think to myself, *oh, why didn't I think of that? Next time I'm in school and someone is mean and says, "Hey, Freckles, you're ugly," I can just look them in the eye and say, "Those aren't freckles. Those are angel kisses, dude."* Give me a break.

REMEMBER, SOMETIMES THE HIGHER THE WALL ON THE OUTSIDE, THE DEEPER THE PAIN ON THE INSIDE.

I never wanted to be known as a motivational speaker, yet that is how many people refer to me. For some, the term "motivational speaker" conjures images of a greasy-haired guy who lives in a van down by the river, out of touch with society and what people are really going through. Still, as a motivational youth speaker, I'm supposed to be optimistic, positive and look at the bright side of life. For the most part I think I do, but I'm also a realist. It is reported that one out of four girls and one out of six boys will be sexually abused by the time they turn 18.[2] I have seen how addiction to drugs and alcohol destroys lives. I understand the impact divorce and dysfunctional homes can have on people. I understand at a deep level what happens emotionally inside.

To simply tell people to be positive isn't going to motivate or change anyone, let alone take away their pain. I want to prove to others they can have an unshakable identity.

I've heard other motivational speakers try to address this. Their face is almost glowing and their step is light as they clasp their hands together and say with a syrupy tone, "Today, I'm going to talk to you about self-esteem and how you can feel good about *you*!" Eyes in the audience begin to roll back in their heads as the speaker points to individuals in the crowd. "Oh, yes," he says, "you and you, and even you, all you need to do first thing each morning when you wake up is go and look in the mirror and … "

Stop. In my book that's mistake number one. I don't know what you look like when you wake up in the morning, but the *last* place I want to look is in the mirror.

The motivational speaker continues, "Look into that mirror and say to yourself five times—not four, not three, not two, or one, but five times—'I am special. I am special. I am special. I am special. I AM SPECIAL.'"

Isn't that *special*? Don't get me wrong. I do believe we're valuable, worthwhile and have dignity no one can take away, but I want something for real life, not just something to be said from a stage or written for a book that sits on a shelf. I want something real, relevant and something I can do right now.

As I mentioned earlier, I played football in high school. We had a great team and actually never lost until the final playoff game. I played tackle. Tom was the guard who played next to me. He was six feet tall and 200 pounds. Imagine if I missed my block and I heard him yell, "Lenz, you're a loser. You blew it." What was I supposed to say? "Hey, I'm not a loser. I'M SPECIAL." Seriously?

I want something that works with the problems and pains of real life.

Growing up I always wanted to change my ears. I think I have a huge ears. Let's face it, sometimes kids can be cruel. Comments like "Dumbo, did you gain any weight this week?" were common for me growing up. To me, those words hurt worse than sticks and stones.

When I was in high school my mom was always telling me to get my hair cut. The mom version of the "in" haircut of the day was given by a guy we called "Carl, the butcher"—I mean, barber. All he needed was a hair trimmer. Truth be told, it seemed more like a weed whacker for your head. It would go down to the skin, up the neck and around the ears. The only time he used a scissors was to cut your bangs above your forehead. It was the world's first mini-Mohawk, which, even if it were in style, didn't look the best on me. The haircut made my ears look even bigger.

I'll never forget the time my mom sent me to get a haircut but, instead, I took the money and went to a store and bought candy. When I got home Mom looked at me curiously and said, "It doesn't look like they took anything off." "What do you mean?" I replied, trying to sound as convincing as possible. "They took an inch off the side and two off the back." "Well," she said suspiciously, "I guess it looks okay."

That's when I started to grow my hair long to cover my ears.

After my hair had grown out quite a bit I was on a retreat where we were supposed to open up and share something really deep. So, I opened up to a girl and shared my insecurity about the size of my ears.

"You think you have big ears? No way," she said. She lifted my hair to see my ears and repeated, "You don't have big ears."

In disbelief, I said, "Come on, really? You don't think I have big ears?" "No," she responded.

I couldn't believe it. Did I just hear right? "You *really* don't think I have big ears?" I asked with hope. "No," she replied. "They match your nose."

What? No one ever told me before that I had a big nose. Oh, great, I could hide my ears with my hair, but what was I going to do now? Grow my hair over my face, try to grow an inverted mustache? Some people thought it was a good idea.

NO, I had to find a way to be okay with ME. I had to stand up against society's system without fists, guns or destructive words. If you look at school shootings or extreme bullying, you'll see revenge at the core. Hurting people hurt people.

I had to find a way to stop the hurting, a way to let the hurting make me a better person instead of eating away at me. I had to find a way to fight the system, not people. I had to stand up against the views and beliefs that were the driving force behind it all.

We can have an unshakable identity and have the personal power to do the next right thing. It's never too late to do the right thing.

As I mentioned, no matter where I go people want to change things about themselves. One of the most common things people want to change is their weight. It seems there's always someone on a diet. They search magazines and the Internet for the perfect weight loss program: "How to lose 50 pounds or more in two days or less. Just buy this product. Just take this little pill." The reality is, typically these unhealthy "diets" don't work. The sad thing is many are still trying them.

Today the trend is to be bigger, faster and stronger, which has brought another drug of choice into popularity: steroids. I honestly wish I could tell you they never work, but it seems they do— temporarily. I saw a photo in a sports magazine of a scrawny little guy. In the article it told how the teenager always wanted to play football and get the attention from girls that football players always seemed to get. He believed it was impossible—until steroids.

The next photo in the magazine was shocking. It was hard to believe it was the same guy. Oh, was he built: bulging arms, a huge neck and a big chest with bulging "pecs." He was wearing a football jersey and, sure enough, girls surrounded him.

There was something perplexing about the photo, though. You couldn't see the number on his jersey because it was covered. Flowers, handwritten letters and snapshots of his life were all around him. The photo in the magazine was not one of him celebrating a victory after a game. It was one of him lying in a casket—dead, according to his obituary a death attributed to steroids.

Do you know how I think that obituary should have read?

Cause of death: drugs, steroids. Mark another valuable human being gone forever because of drug abuse. Then, the obituary should have continued with *reason* for death: no sense of identity/searching for identity/low self-esteem. I have to wonder if it was bullying that pushed him over the edge.

We can't just focus on drugs like steroids or even prescription drug abuse, because more people die as a result of alcohol abuse than all other drugs combined.[3] Still, it's true the *cause* of his death was drugs or steroids, but that wasn't the only *reason* for his death. Perhaps it included no sense of identity. Perhaps he felt he couldn't be himself, that his best wasn't good enough, that he had to be in a different group or clique to measure up. He believed if he could just be a star football player then he'd be somebody and belong somewhere.

He looked to *something* to try to change who he was.

Searching for a secure identity will never be listed as a cause of death, but thousands of people are literally dying every day because of it. Suicide remains the third leading cause of death among teens, and claims more than 38,000 lives each year, the equivalent of 105 people per day. On average, one suicide occurs every four to five minutes. In the time it has taken you to read this chapter, several people have given up on life. But an even harsher reality is that over 487,700 people are either hospitalized or treated in the emergency room each year for suicide attempts that failed, meaning that more than 1,300 people attempt suicide every day. Suicide is only exceeded by accidents and homicide as leading causes of death among teens.[4]

What is a contributing factor to the top three causes of death among teens? Low self-worth.

Every time I speak at a school I meet teenagers who struggle with anorexia, bulimia or obesity. It's another sign of how society and the media continue to convince people that who they are isn't good enough. In 2013, Americans spent over $60 billion on dieting and diet-related products in an effort to eat less and lose weight.[5] That's billions more dollars than the U.S. Government budgets for global humanitarian aid to feed those who are truly hungry.[6]

Something's wrong with the system. The unrealistic expectations society has created aren't working. Instead, we've been convinced it's more important to spend money trying to starve ourselves than it is to spend money feeding those who are starving.

Why do we need a Dignity Revolution? Society's system isn't working.

ON AVERAGE, ONE SUICIDE OCCURS EVERY FOUR TO FIVE MINUTES. IN THE TIME IT HAS TAKEN YOU TO READ THIS CHAPTER, SEVERAL PEOPLE HAVE GIVEN UP ON LIFE.

CHAPTER 5

THE SYSTEM ISN'T FAIR

REASON 2

The second reason we need to stand up against society's system and have a Dignity Revolution is because of what society says we have to have, or be, or do to feel good isn't fair.

I've tried to draw a bell for you. Note I said, "Tried." I never got an *A* in art; I never got a *B* in art; I never even got a *C* or *D* in art class.

You might need to use your imagination, but let's say my drawing of this bell represents society. Just like society itself, this bell isn't perfect. Imagine there is a section of this bell representing 10 percent of society. Some people in society's system call this portion gifted.

If a guy is seven feet tall in America, you assume he might be gifted at basketball, right? During training, the coach tells him, "See the basket? See the ball? Put the ball in the basket." So, the guy dribbles the ball downcourt, jumps, makes a slam-dunk and everyone cheers. I'm not sure why people get so excited about it, though. The guy is so tall he could probably slam-dunk the ball without jumping at all.

When I was in high school a lot of people said I was gifted at football. The coach would say to me, "Hey, Bob, see the guy with the ball?"

"Yeah," I'd reply.

"He's the quarterback."

"Oh," I'd say.

The coach continued, "See the guy in the other color?"

"Color? Uh-huh," I'd reply.

"You need to stop him."

So, I asked the coach how and he responded, "Stand in his way. It's called blocking."

"Oh, okay." Actually, I was pretty good at blocking.

Am I cutting down sports? No. If you are gifted in those areas, live it out to your full potential, drug and alcohol free. What I am asking, though, is this: Is a guy gifted just because he's seven feet tall, or am I gifted because I'm seven feet wide? Perhaps not, and it's unfair to make those assumptions. The reason I don't think it's fair is because the system bases giftedness on the externals, a bunch of what I call the "P's" of society:

*P*hysical appearance, what you look like
*P*erformance, how well you do or how successful you are
*P*ossessions, the clothes you wear, the car you drive or the house you own
*P*opularity, how many friends you have
*P*leasure, doing what you want, when you want, because it feels good
*P*restige, how recognized or respected you are
*P*ower, how much influence you have over others

No matter which school I visit, I inevitably see a certain group of guys huddled together, leaning against their lockers in the hallway checking out the girls and making rude comments. I used to think it was just guys discriminating against girls, but I've been on enough campuses to see how the girls respond when a cute guy walks by. Girls just do it a bit differently.

Making comments like these is not fair, and the reason it's not fair is because it's still basing the other person's value on the externals, the outside. A system like this bases identity only on what you have, what you look like and what you can do.

If 10 percent is somehow deemed more important because of their giftedness, then I propose there is another 10 percent of society just as unique, just as human, just as important. Society sometimes calls them handicapped, mentally challenged or special needs persons.

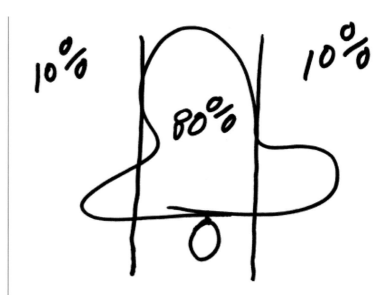

Society's system was demonstrated to me on a plane returning from a speaking engagement. As I walked onto the plane, to my left I saw the cockpit where the pilot would sit. When I turned the corner to my right, near the front of the plane I saw these large seats that looked like recliners. *Yes,* I thought, *finally a seat that fits.*

The seat wasn't for me, however. It was for someone who "possessed" something I didn't: lots of money. The seat was for a little lady with a briefcase. She sat down, with enough room for two more of her. It was the first-class section, made up of a small percentage of the seats on the plane. I had to go to the back of the plane where the majority of the travelers had to sit: second class. Of course, they didn't call it that. It wouldn't sell if they did. They called it coach class.

I got to my seat and thought *do they seriously expect me to fit into that?* As I slid into the small seat you could almost hear the squeaking sound of my body squeezing into position. If you think getting in was difficult, you should have seen me trying to get out. A crowbar would have helped, but they wouldn't allow one on the plane.

There was another 10 percent on the plane that day: luggage. The airline didn't handle it with much care. They mostly just threw the luggage into the baggage area. Passengers used to be able to bring along a free bag, but now most airlines charge for luggage. If you check in late, or use carry-on luggage to avoid an extra charge, and if the carry-on is too big or weighs too much, it might have to be moved to the baggage area of the plane, holding up the flight. The excess baggage is a problem that needs to be eliminated.

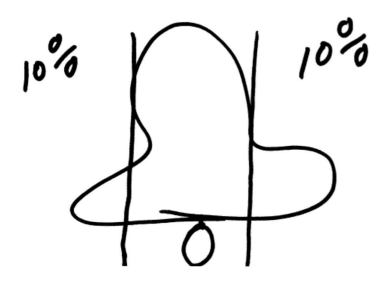

That leaves 80 percent who are average or *normal,* a bad word nowadays.

Like society's system, the airlines consider some people who have the right stuff to be worthy of special treatment: first-class. The majority of passengers are just average, run-of-the-mill travelers: coach. What about luggage, the stuff that doesn't quite fit in with the other passengers? Well, it is just considered baggage that is thrown out of sight, out of mind. Or worse, some believe we should eliminate the excess baggage all together.

In some ways I think society's system works the same way. Some people may be considered gifted because they have a good body, nice hair, a clear complexion, good grades, or are good in sports. Those are all good things, and I'm not saying we shouldn't pursue them.

But what happens if, for some reason, you don't have those qualities? Or worse yet, what if you don't even fit into the average category? What then? Does that mean you're just luggage and if there isn't room, you should be eliminated? I don't think so.

Any system that says some people are gifted and other people are just "luggage" to be eliminated is a system I don't believe is fair.

I have a friend who would fall into this category. Not only is she a friend, but she's my sister. My sister's name is Lois and she has special needs. She is mentally challenged. If you say, "Shut up," in my house, you'll hear Lois respond, "Oh, that's not nice." She's so innocent. She's so awesome.

As I shared embarrassing moments before, I failed to mention one involving Lois. You'll soon understand why I hesitated to share it.

Like many small towns, in my hometown, the private and public middle schools came together to form one school for high school. As a freshman, I was with a new group of guys trying to make new friends, and I invited them to our family's cottage. We were all having a great time together water skiing and swimming.

After the water activities, we gathered around the picnic table to play cards. All of a sudden, I noticed Lois coming toward us from the cottage. My friends had never met her and she was doing something embarrassing to me. I tried to get her to stop by holding up my hand, but she couldn't see me. Her handicap has severely affected her eyesight that glasses cannot correct. So, she kept walking toward us.

What embarrassed me was what she was wearing over the top of her head, nose and mouth. It was an athletic supporter. There I was with my new friends trying to fit in, when Lois came walking up with it stretched over her face like a mask you'd see worn in an operating room. Panic gripped me. If that wasn't bad enough, Lois said, "You guys wanna play doctor?"

I cringed and braced for my friends' reactions. They weren't sure how to react, whether to laugh or not. One of them asked, "Bob, who is this?"

I'm ashamed to tell you I didn't stand up for my sister. I struggled with my own identity and wanted to fit in so badly. "I don't know," I said. "It must be some neighbor girl my mom is taking care of."

I denied she was my own sister. I made believe I didn't know her. I didn't have enough guts to stand up against the system. I didn't have enough guts to stand up for the dignity, worth and beauty of my own flesh and blood. I thought the approval of my friends was life to me. I'll never forget the guilt and emotional turmoil I felt by denying my relationship with my own sister.

Never again will I deny Lois the dignity she deserves. That's why I speak, and that's why I'm writing this book. Every person has value. No one deserves to be bullied, harassed, put down, mocked, or made to feel alone or worthless. And no one deserves to feel abandoned, invisible or rejected like I rejected my sister that day.

If you're not willing to stand up against the system, would you please tell my sister she's not valuable or gifted? Would somebody please have enough courage to say, "Lois, I'm sorry, you don't have what it takes. Lois, you don't have a nice body, a clear complexion or nice hair. Lois, you're not very intelligent and you'll never go to college. You'll never have a boyfriend, never drive a car and you'll never own a home. Lois, you're just not valuable."

Would you say, "Lois, I hate to tell you this, but not only are you not gifted, you're not even normal. According to society's system for determining self-worth, you're nothing but luggage. Lois, if we get too much luggage, if we get too many handicapped people in society, it's going to drain us financially and become a burden. You know what happens to excess luggage, don't you? We'll simply have to eliminate some. We'll just call it mercy killing, because what kind of an identity can a retarded person have anyway?"

Sounds harsh, doesn't it? Obviously, this is not meant to be taken literally, but to make a point. Who would ever say such a thing? I love the campaigns to get rid of the "R" word. But believe it or not, as I've traveled around the world I've actually met people who have said they would say these words to Lois. Some have joked, but others have said with complete sincerity, "I'll tell her because it's true."

It seems hard to believe anyone being so cruel, but it's more common than we'd like to admit. This kind of societal system and belief has been demonstrated in other ways throughout history. This type of societal system is unacceptable and unfair, and I fear if the system isn't reversed through a Dignity Revolution, it may continue.

CHAPTER 6

T4: THE SYSTEM DEHUMANIZES PEOPLE

REASON 3

The third reason we need to have a Dignity Revolution and stand up to society's current system of determining self-worth is because it dehumanizes people.

Bullying strips people of their dignity. It devalues human beings. It takes advantage of the weak. This is not a new phenomenon in society and we can't let history repeat itself.

Some of you might say, "Easier said than done." You may wonder how standing up to the system is possible when life experiences have sent a message saying, "You're worthless." How can you believe you have value when society says, "You don't measure up"? For some, the actions of their own family and friends scream, "You don't matter." Fathers have walked out of their kids' lives. Mothers have turned their heads, pretending to not see the abuse. The very person you used to call your best friend taunts and bullies you after school.

You feel tried and tested, worthless, unfulfilled and invisible.

Most often the values a society lives by and is known for come from what the people in that society deem important and, unfortunately, this might lead to being a prisoner versus a product of society. These values often establish the ideals of life, its circumstances, behaviors and responses. When something isn't deemed valuable we throw it away, disregard it or say it's good-for-nothing.

What exactly is value?

Value \ val-( )yü\ **noun** *1: worth, merit, or importance*
Value verb *1: to consider with respect, excellence, or usefulness; 2: to regard or esteem highly*

In our environmentally conscious society, we have seen the need to reuse and recycle. It's sad to say the same society that finds value or worth in trash has left so many people feeling completely worthless. What standards are we using to determine the self-worth of so many people? And why are so many feeling worthless, like they have failed the test of life?

I believe our system places a higher value on things (what you own), appearance (what you look like), talent (athletic, intellectual or musical abilities), pleasure (having a good time) and influence (power and control), rather than the intrinsic worth and dignity of each human being. How you treat someone is based on the value you place on them. When society values things more than people, it sees others and themselves as disposable.

Society's problems and social ills come when a philosophy or core belief considers ideology, progress, achievements, products or finances more important than people, more important than love, more important than relationships. This system reduces people to products.

People are to be cherished and loved, not used. Things are to be used, not cherished and loved. The system has it backwards.

Our system often declares unless you're at the top you have no value. Even human life is cast aside when it doesn't fit into someone's plan for success.

The disintegration of value can range from picking on kids in the cafeteria to terrorism, from name-calling to school shootings, from feeling pressured to having name-brand clothing to rejecting someone based on the color of their skin or their gender. It may appear as graffiti on school walls or through the inhumane treatment of gay students, from the dismantling of any right or wrong to the eradication of life under Hitler.

You might be thinking, "Aren't you taking this a little far by comparing society's system for determining self-worth to Hitler's reign in Nazi Germany?"

Let's explore.

A philosophy declaring certain people more valuable to society than others is what Hitler lived by. His reign wasn't by chance, but driven by a worldview he pieced together from different schools of thought. Studying it, you'll see traces of Nietzsche, Wagner, Greek pagan mythology, Darwin and other German thinkers who preceded him with a goal to improve the genetic quality of the human race. He even took parts of Christian thought and distorted them to meet his agenda. Hitler twisted religion to promote racism, prejudice and hatred to an extreme the world had never experienced. Hitler believed an entire group of people, an entire race (the Jews), were inferior. It was this core belief that fueled Hitler's desire to destroy them, to wipe them off the face of the earth.

So, Hitler began what has become known as the Holocaust, resulting in the eradication of approximately six million Jews. Their crime? It was their heritage, their bloodline, their religion and their appearance. That's right, their crime included the color of their skin and eyes. Hitler believed the Aryan man was superior—blond hair and blue eyes were best. I have always thought it was ridiculous since he had black hair and that famous mustache. Still, he felt the Jews were inferior to the Aryans and their bloodline was infected, impure and not worthy of life. He believed we should be genetically selective, that some people were not only better at some tasks, but more intelligent and ultimately had more value. He believed in the "preservation of the most-favorite species," the Aryan, white, Caucasian human.

In an attempt to prove it genetically, Hitler wanted to show the effects socially and socioeconomically. He believed he could elimi-nate poverty if these "blemishes of society" were removed. He wanted and preached a new race, a second Adam, a perfect society, an ideal person, a superman, if you will. In Hitler's mind, it would only be possible if he could rid the world of Jews. He implied they didn't have a *right* to exist.

In 1919, Hitler served as a corporal in World War I and was wounded. While in the hospital he claimed to have had a vision believing he was the chosen one to bring Germany back to victory after the disappointing news they had lost the war. He depicted Jews as a worthless drain on the economy. He was convinced, and therefore was able to convince many people, that the Jews were the problem with Germany and the world.

Imagine someone condemning an entire race as the problem with the world today, forging a campaign against a whole ethnic group or nation; for example, the Dutch, Muslims, Asians, Africans, Christians or Latinos. Imagine the goal was to wipe them out, to purge the world of them completely. We shudder at the thought; yet that was Hitler's aim. His target was the Jewish people. But what many people don't realize is that it didn't start there.

As a prelude to his attempts to eliminate the Jews, Hitler began a campaign to eliminate others he believed were inferior, of no worth or less than important, who didn't measure up to his values. There were hundreds of thousands of people other than Jews who were killed, terminated, wiped out and murdered under his dominion. In fact, those whose mindset justified targeting these other groups of people did not believe it was wrong. They believed it was the right and good thing to do.

To them, it was not murder. To them, it couldn't be murder if the other group of people they targeted were less than human and had no value. They declared they were not real people, but mistakes … accidents … problems … like a pebble in the shoe or thorn in the side … a hindrance to success … undignified. By getting rid of them, Hitler believed he was doing Germany and the world a favor, a service to country and to those in the religious establishment who preached against Jews, gypsies and heretics, which had been ongoing for centuries.

It is so sad when people use religion to defend crimes against humanity. History continues to repeat itself, from genocide still happening today to the mistreatment of other groups of people because of their race, gender, wealth, status, orientation, religion or political views.

Hundreds of thousands more were dead. Why? Because they didn't fit the ideal of what their society deemed "good." Those under Hitler's reign developed a list of over 20 different groups they deemed not valuable. Who fell into this category? Who did Hitler consider less than human? Among them: gypsies, the Slavic and Polish people, Soviet prisoners of war, homosexuals, Christians who would not pledge their allegiance to Hitler, and Germans (yes, even Germans) who were of no "use" to them, like the elderly and the handicapped—like my sister, Lois. Under Hitler's rule, my sister would have been exterminated.

Hitler's code name for the program to eradicate these people: T4, the *other* Holocaust.

"What? I don't remember reading about T4 in my history books. Why have I never heard of this?" These are questions you may be asking. Today, you can easily look it up online and read about Dr. Karl Brandt who conducted human experiments and euthanized countless victims. He was one of Hitler's doctors who headed up the T4 Euthanasia Program. He was later convicted of war crimes against humanity and executed in June 1948.

I didn't learn about this in school either. The first time I became aware of it was when I toured the United States Holocaust Memorial Museum in Washington, D.C., a place I think everyone should visit. I entered a section with a display titled "T4."

There I learned T4 was an abbreviation based on the address in Berlin where the headquarters for the program were located: Tiergartenstrasse 4. It's there they ordered experiments on the elderly, the physically and mentally handicapped, the institutionalized or anyone considered genetically inferior.

Hear me. This is fact. I did the research. This isn't ancient history. This is just a little more than 70 years ago. There are Holocaust survivors still alive today who witnessed these atrocities. May their stories never be forgotten.

When I share the story of T4 as I travel, I rarely meet anyone in the audience who has heard of it. One person, however, Dr. Jake Jacobs, a professor whose degrees include Judeo-Christian studies, did know about it and gave me much insight and many resources for research. I have now vowed to educate as many people as I can on the reality of T4.

The realities are hard to believe. Disabled children were removed from their homes and families and taken to "special" hospitals, where an arm and a leg would be cut off and surgically exchanged just to see what would happen. Other experiments and exterminations were done using gas, suffocation, lethal injections, poisonings and overdoses of medications just to see how much the human body could tolerate before succumbing to death.

For example, they would starve a person just to see how long they could live without food or water. They would measure how long a person could "last" and then document the stages of starvation. They placed children underwater to see how long it would take before they drowned. They did air pressure tests to see what heights people could withstand before their eyes popped out. If they were not killed it was mandatory for those whom they considered genetically inferior to be sterilized to prevent their bloodline from "infecting" the next generation. We would not instill such cruelties on an animal.

PEOPLE ARE TO BE CHERISHED AND LOVED, NOT USED. THINGS ARE TO BE USED, NOT CHERISHED AND LOVED.

The torture was horrific and seemingly unbelievable. But again, it happened in modern history. T4 had a slogan used as propaganda to try and justify the program. It was a slogan that became synonymous with T4: "Life unworthy of life."

Did you catch it? The very motto used to rationalize and defend the acts of T4 was "life unworthy of life." They literally believed it.

How could so many people be so blind and not see this evil when it is so obvious to us today? It reminds me of a famous quote:

When Hitler came for the Jews, I was not a Jew,
therefore I was not concerned.
And when Hitler attacked the Catholics, I was not a Catholic,
and therefore, I was not concerned.
And when Hitler attacked the unions and industrialists,
I was not a member of the unions, and I was not concerned.
Then, Hitler attacked me and the Protestant church,
and there was nobody left to be concerned.[1]

Martin Niemöller, 1892-1984
German theologian and pastor

I've pictured in my mind, maybe from the movies I've seen, row after row of men in the Nazi army. They were *real* people: fathers, brothers, sons and friends, marching in unison, seemingly without thought, to the beat of a madman's drum. I've seen documentaries where Hitler approached to address the soldiers with massive crowds gathered. Everyone stopped and stood at attention in his presence, listening to his every word as if it were a cure to disease.

But here's the thing. I believe their longings were legitimate. Their yearning was for a new way, a new life and a better life. Their yearning was for some good news. This is a natural desire that cannot and should not be questioned. But I still have to ask, where was their conscience? Where was their common sense, much less rational thought? They seemed mesmerized, as if in a trance. How could they be such fools? How could they not notice in their longing for a more true, more pure humankind, that they were now anything but "human *kind*?" They turned into animals themselves.

Why didn't people see it? Surely, the church and human rights activists didn't bow to Hitler's lies. Yes, there were some who didn't, including Dietrich Bonhoeffer and others. But sadly, most were either silent, caved in fear or bowed on bended knee at the false promise of power, position, safety and security. They hoped for a better life rather than standing for the *dignity* of all people. Friends turned their backs on neighbors when they saw the yellow Star of David marking them as Jews, marking them as damaged goods.

I've never heard it spoken live, but it still rings in my head from the documentaries I've seen—"Heil Hitler! Heil Hitler!" Crowds of people pledged their allegiance, devotion, time, energy and family, giving him their trust and their very lives. It's a salutation for a king (as in "hail to the king"). Actually, to kings who viewed themselves as gods, "Heil Hitler" was more than a declaration. It was like a prayer, a holy vow like that of ordination into the ministry, as if giving one's heart in deepest worship. Their salute of word and action, an arm raised high in the air, was their sign of devotion.

Their pledge for all to hear and see declared their life as his to do with as he willed. "Heil Hitler" or "You have all rights to me. I'm yours. I submit to your reign, your kingdom, your worldview and your philosophy. It is not my life."

How could they?

It seems so clear in hindsight. Like me, are you thinking *we surely would have stood against it, right*? Even now if I asked, "Do you believe Hitler was right?" I can almost hear you shouting, "NO, NO." My heart joins with you, bursting with a resounding "NO, of course not."

Many will say they hate war, all war, especially those that do not seem to fit anyone's criteria for a "just war." But, oh, even many who disdain war still offer a "hats off" and heart of gratitude to the men and women who fought to free the world of the rule of this despicable regime and its philosophy in World War II.

I often share something with groups of people and it makes them cringe and causes defenses to go up, way up. It's the mere suggestion that certain areas in America's value system are remotely similar to Hitler's horrible agenda.

As you can imagine, when I share the T4 story with groups, there is always an uneasy feeling in the room, a dark cloud of disgust and outrage. You see, we are made to stand up against evil. We are designed to cheer for justice and against injustice. The mere suggestion we may hold some of the same detestable philosophies as did Hitler's regime about the value of life goes against something deep inside us.

Still, can you deny we live in a throwaway society where many people believe some of these very things at the core, oftentimes about themselves? Connect the dots. See the painting on the wall. Let's pull our heads out of the sand. I wish it weren't true, but the theory of T4 is alive and well in America today.

"Life unworthy of life."

"How?" you say.

Every year we lose more than 38,000 Americans to suicide[2] because they've been convinced their life has no meaning or significance. They've been convinced their life is unworthy of life.

We lost nearly 3,000 lives on September 11, 2001, to terrorism.[3] May we never forget that tragedy—the horror, the fear, the loss, the families affected, the pain or the images of those planes crashing into the World Trade Center towers and the Pentagon. Many efforts have been made to protect Americans from terrorism since then, including a defense budget of nearly $550 billion each year. Yes, 10 zeros: $550,000,000,000.[4] But I have to ask, "What are we doing to protect our children from the terrorist inside our own borders, inside our own skin, the terrorist of low self-esteem?"

Nearly 3,000 lives were lost on 9/11. Yet more than *10 times* as many were lost to suicide in the same year, and every year since. Do the math. For every 10 years, there are another 380,000 or so lives lost to suicide. This is a tragedy of epic proportions. Where are the headlines? Where are the news reports?

Truth is, what society's system told us we needed to have, be, or do to feel good about ourselves is a lie. We need to stand up against it.

REAL INTEGRITY IS FOUND WHEN YOU CARE FOR THE DIGNITY OF EVERY PERSON, EVEN THE PERSON YOU DISAGREE WITH THE MOST.

Estimates show 12 to 23 percent of adolescents engage in self-injury,[5] most commonly in the form of cutting. When asked why they do it multiple times a day, many will say the pain caused from cutting is *nothing* compared to their emotional pain. The bearable pain of self-injury becomes a distraction from the unbearable pain going on deep inside. It's another wall to hide the hurt, a wall that quickly becomes a seemingly inescapable prison.

There are many prisoners of war in our society. It's a cultural war, fought with images coming in at a rate too great and fast to be precise. In fact, many of the images aren't even real, having been Photoshopped and altered beyond the point of recognition. Magazines are full of erased wrinkles and blemishes, reduced waistlines and enhanced muscles. We're a nation convinced we need to have faster cars, better jobs, higher pay, fuller lips, smaller hips, fewer wrinkles, bigger muscles, thicker hair, better grades, busy schedules, and the list goes on and on. So many have bought into the system telling us if we don't achieve these things, then we're somehow less human, less worthy of life.

Every time you believe and give in to the message, "If I were richer, thinner, prettier, stronger, smarter or more popular, then I'd be okay," you're saying, "Hail to the system of T4." Are we too blind to see what it's doing to us? Are we afraid to take on the system? Or, are we in a daze, mesmerized not by Hitler but by Hollywood? Are we influenced, not by chance, but by well-thought-out, pieced-together philosophies of the past, modern and postmodern thinkers who preached, "Let's make a show of the survival of the fittest."

Let's find the common sense to recognize the philosophies and power ruling over us today, and find the courage to fight against them.

To further research T4, I went to Germany with my son, David, and toured a Holocaust museum. It had to be difficult for them to portray the events and mistakes of their own nation, but they wanted to show the realities of it in hopes it would never happen again. It was heartbreaking. The ache in my soul and pain in my stomach comes back every time I think of it. We also toured sites of concentration camps and saw where people were gassed, and the furnaces where their bodies were burned. We walked along the ditches once filled with their corpses, and along the river where their ashes were later thrown to hide any evidence.

But there was no mention of T4. So, I called several tour guides. Not one of them even knew what T4 stood for, much less offered a historical tour. When I recalled that T4 stood for Tiergartenstrasse 4, the address where the atrocities were planned and organized, David and I decided to go there on our own. We walked up and down the street searching and couldn't believe there wasn't anything to mark this place of such historic relevance. I expected a monument or museum. Finally, we came upon it: a small plaque set in the pavement and a sign indicating where the original building once stood. My son and I stood stunned and in disbelief. This is it?

Forbid that they, or we, ever forget a philosophy claiming that any life, like my sister's, or yours or mine for that matter, is not worthy of life.

Yet, I see it every day. The ache in my soul and pain in my gut I felt while touring the Holocaust museum is the same feeling I get when hearing stories of some of the young people who talk with me after a school assembly program—like the kid from a special needs class who shared how others called him retarded and made fun of him. He shared that the class would probably be his favorite, but he didn't like going because he felt so bad about himself when people made fun of him and put him down—or the sharp-looking, redheaded kid with freckles all over his face who came up to me. I only saw pain in his eyes, reminding me of a victim of war, which wasn't far from reality for him. People ridiculed and laughed at him, calling him a faggot. While waiting at the bus stop, kids would throw rocks and make fun of him. He felt like he was alone. "What do I do?" he asked. "How do I deal with it when they call me these names"?

Then a senior in high school came up to me. He began crying. "I didn't expect to come to an assembly program today," he said, "but it's what I needed so bad." Tears streamed down his face as he began crying uncontrollably. "I had a horrible weekend," he continued. "Six of the jocks in school followed me to my car and called me names and kept ridiculing me and calling me gay, and they beat me up." My heart sank as I watched his pain-filled face. "But the worst thing was when no one would stop the junior high kid from spitting on me."

No one, no one deserves to be treated like this. May we be the ones leading the way to a Dignity Revolution by seeking out opportunities to love, understand, invite, care, defend and stand for justice. May we be the ones to stand up against a system that has deemed those who are different as unworthy of our respect, kindness or friendship. Real integrity is found when you care for the dignity of every person, even the person you disagree with the most.

There's an ache in my soul when I hear stories of youth who have been bullied and feel worthless because they're mocked for how they look, for who they are, or for what they can or can't do. No one should ever get to the point where they view death as more appealing than life.

This is wrong. This is injustice. No one, for any reason, should ever be bullied or stripped of their dignity. We need to declare, not just with lip service, but with our actions toward one another, that Hitler was wrong. We need to rebel against the T4 message of "life unworthy of life" in any way, shape or form, not just as part of a history lesson, but as a vital declaration for today. We need to declare every life is worthy of life. Can we topple this regime and this system? Or, are we too tightly in its grip?

MAY WE BE THE ONES LEADING THE WAY TO A DIGNITY REVOLUTION BY SEEKING OUT OPPORTUNITIES TO LOVE, UNDERSTAND, INVITE, CARE, DEFEND AND STAND FOR JUSTICE.

CHAPTER 7

WHAT IS CONTROLLING US?

REASON 4

We've explored the first three reasons to stand up against society's system, but before we talk about this last reason, I have some questions:

What *system?*
What *philosophy?*
What *values?*
What *belief system?*
What *is predominant in us?*
What *governs our thoughts?*
What *captivates our attention?*
What *invades our minds as we're lying in bed or during downtime?*
What *dictates how we view others and ourselves?*
What *is important or essential in seeing someone as worthwhile?*

These are questions of life. What system does each of us live by for determining self-worth? What controls our thoughts and feelings, and therefore our actions? How do we treat people? What structural system have we allowed to be in place in our society, one that walks all over the dignity of so many people?

We have to recognize what's controlling real life.

I can't imagine anyone responding *yes* to a survey or questionnaire asking if Hitler was right, other than perhaps a neo-Nazi extremist. I have spoken with people who lived in Germany during the rule of Hitler in World War II who were unaware of the extent of his actions. They were horrified when they learned about them and would never have approved.

Perhaps our "ignorance" and unwillingness to strip away the masks and truly look at ourselves as well as society is the first part of the problem. If we know something is not right, say nothing or turn the other way, aren't we just another silent bystander allowing it to go on? Aren't we then just as guilty? When I walked by Jack, my teammate hanging from the fence post at my school, and didn't do anything to help him, I was just as guilty as those who put him there.

We have a responsibility to each other as fellow human beings in this world we live in. We know many people are damaging or throwing their lives away to drugs, self-harm, suicide and a host of other unhealthy choices. Though we may not know the cause(s), we have a responsibility to ask questions: Why are you hurting? Why do you feel worthless? Then, it's our responsibility to do something about it.

It's so much easier in hindsight to condemn the actions of others in theory, in the past, or as part of a history book. But we are writing history with every choice we make and action we take, and we must look to where the rubber meets the road.

Let's review the reasons we need to stand up to society's system and become part of a Dignity Revolution.

REASON 1 | THE SYSTEM ISN'T WORKING.

We talked about a system for determining self-worth or dignity based on what society most often says we need to have, be or do to feel good about ourselves. We know that nine out of 10 people want to change something about themselves and more than 1,300 people a day attempt suicide. We know the old system of "externals" or the seven "P's" don't work. Society's system tells us we need to look a certain way, act a certain way, and be beautiful, intelligent, successful, athletic, popular or rich in order to be someone. The chart that follows demonstrates society's *old system* as opposed to what a Dignity Revolution can do to create a *new system*.

OLD SYSTEM Identity based on external qualities	NEW SYSTEM Identity based on internal qualities of love
PHYSICAL APPEARANCE Have the perfect body and clear complexion.	**CHARACTER** Know who you are as a whole person.
POPULARITY Know the right people. Be part of the "right" group(s).	**COURAGE** Stand up for what is right and what you believe.
POWER Who or what must I influence and control?	**COMPASSION** Concern for others as well as self. Strive for justice.
PLEASURE Have what you want, when you want, because it feels good.	**COMMITMENT** Stand by friends through adversity. Keep promises and overcome differences.
PERFORMANCE Excel for attention and praise.	**CONSISTENCY** Live life without hypocrisy. Support words with action.
PRESTIGE Have the right job. Live in the right part of town.	**CREATIVITY** Celebrate individuality and use unique talents to benefit the wider community.
POSSESSIONS Wear the right clothes and drive the right car to impress others.	**CHARITY** Love life and others as well as yourself.

REASON 2 | THE SYSTEM ISN'T FAIR.

Would you tell my sister, Lois, that she's not gifted or worthy of respect or love because she doesn't fit into the "normal" category? Is it really fair to base her worth and dignity on the seven "P's"? Lois thinks she is gifted. Lois has a great identity. She would never throw her life away to drugs, alcohol, anorexia, cutting, sex or suicide. She believes she's beautiful, gifted and valuable. And so do I. She's proud of who she is. And so am I.

Society's system tells us our identity is based only on externals, like what you possess, how you look, what you know or who you know. It leaves so many people feeling worthless and without value and dignity, like excess luggage to be eliminated.

Would you agree this system is not fair?

REASON 3 | T4: THE SYSTEM DEHUMANIZES PEOPLE.

Any worldview that allows the use of words or actions to treat people as things to be discarded is in danger of repeating history.

I'm going to assume you agree society's system for determining self-worth and dignity is not working, is not fair and dehumanizes people. Yet, can we be honest enough to confess this system is the very system society uses, and the very system we typically live by today?

Are we honest enough to admit this flawed, failed, unjust system is the very same system we have knowingly or unknowingly bought into?

Let me say it loud and clear …

WE CANNOT LET THE SYSTEM WIN. WE CANNOT LET THE BULLIES CONTROL US.

REASON 4 | THE SYSTEM IS CONTROLLING US.

We need to stand up to society's system because this very flawed and unfair system is *controlling* us. It's ruling over us like a cruel king inflicting more and more burdens on his subjects. It's a kingdom stripping people of their rights and dignity.

Most people have to confess, "I didn't realize how I was being controlled by the system." It seems to have us under its spell. Its claws have dug deep. Its thinking permeates the airwaves and dominates themes of our music, movies and media. We have been inundated on every side, submersed in its philosophy. Society's kingdom reigns with an iron fist—a force that runs things, a power that pulls the strings, reducing us to puppets who have lost control. It resides in our culture, and we seem unable to fight it.

Some would say it's even in our very nature. We've accepted it as part of our lives and treat others and ourselves as if we have no dignity. Over 3.2 million young people are being bullied each year. It is estimated that 20 percent of high school students are being bullied at any given time. That's one in five being hit, shoved, taunted or intimidated.[1]

And now smartphones and social networking have provided yet additional environments in which bullying takes place.

We also need to look at all the self-abusive and at-risk behavior, with an estimated 2 million Americans cutting or harming themselves. We can no longer be silent. Too many people feel worthless. We cannot let the system win. We cannot let the bullies control us.

I already shared how in high school I didn't stand up for my sister, Lois, because I was embarrassed. I didn't have the courage to stand up against society's system that controlled me. The truth is, it has controlled me in different ways at different times, and was demonstrated once again involving my sister.

Lois loved to walk around our block every day or ride her adult tricycle on the sidewalk. Such a simple thing brought her so much joy. She wasn't hurting anything or anybody. But we had a neighborhood bully named Sammy who would say mean things to Lois and others. He used inap-

propriate and hurtful words. I will never forget the time he blocked the sidewalk and wouldn't allow my sister to pass. He intimidated and bullied her until she started to cry. She came home shaking and sobbing.

This time, I could no longer keep quiet. I was so angry. This had to be made right. I went to Sammy and asked if he had indeed blocked the sidewalk as Lois said. "Yeah," he told me. "What are you going to do about it?" "I'm going to tell your mom," I said. "Go right ahead," he yelled. I knocked on their door, and after a long awkward wait, Sammy's mom answered it and asked if she could help me.

"Sammy was bullying my sister and wouldn't let her pass by on the sidewalk with her trike. He made her cry." Sammy's mom looked perplexed and said, "Oh, there must be some mistake. My little Sammy would never do something like that." She turned to her son and added, "Would you, Sammy?" Sammy's demeanor had changed from the time I confronted him. It was like Jekyll and Hyde. I almost didn't recognize the innocent boyish expression on his face as he answered, "No, Mom, never." At that, his mother smiled approvingly, turned and retreated into her house. "Now what are you going to do?" laughed Sammy, his innocent demeanor suddenly reverting to a sinister smile.

I couldn't believe what happened. How could his mom be so blind? How could she not care what happened to Lois? How could she just blow it off and not get to the truth?

Yes, my sadness for Lois made me angry when I learned what Sammy did to her, but when the adult in the situation did not take the reporting of bullying seriously and treat the situation with proper consequences, my anger turned to outrage. I remember feeling like I was losing control. I wanted revenge. I looked at Sammy and said, "If you ever hurt my sister again, I'll …"

No matter what I may have spouted off at that point, would you blame me? Well, his actions didn't stop, no big surprise there. That's why it's important for parents, teachers, coaches, adults and peers to take every report of bullying incidents seriously. The bully must have consequences to his or her actions. It cannot be tolerated or ignored.

Sammy struck again, this time taking a staple gun and shooting staples at younger neighborhood kids, as well as Lois. I took matters into my own hands and got some guys together. I wanted Sammy to feel my sister's pain and to pay for what he had done.

When telling this story I've had some people say, "Good for you. He deserved whatever you did to him."

But don't you see? By seeking to harm him, I became just like him. I became the bully. The system was still controlling me. At one time, it controlled me by being silent. This time it controlled me by allowing my anger and rage to own me.

When we retaliate, we become the bully, the one who can get in trouble with the law. Thankfully, standing up to Sammy with a group of friends was enough to have him back down. We can't let anger escalate to violence or the cycle will never stop. If one adult doesn't believe, go to another or to the authorities. You do have a choice and you can stand up for yourself without dehumanizing or hurting another.

Are we going to lower ourselves to the standards of a bully or rise above them? Dr. Martin Luther King Jr. put it another way: "… Darkness cannot drive out darkness: only light can do that. Hate cannot cast out hate: only love can do that." Yes, what Sammy did was wrong, but choosing to either ignore it or fight back with hatred were not the only options.

Some people bully to get attention, to become popular, to push others down in an effort to build themselves up. They feel better about themselves when they feel big or powerful. Others may come from families where there is physical or verbal abuse on a regular basis. They think being angry, calling people names, belittling someone or pushing people around is the normal way of life.

Some of the worst outbreaks of bullying have come from people who have been bullied or ignored. Someone who has been the victim of bullying or abuse is many more times likely to act out in unhealthy ways. They have been made to feel insignificant and small, often turning to self-harm to deal with the emotional pain inside or bullying someone more vulnerable to gain a sense of superiority and identity.

People have blamed everything from suicide to school shootings on bullying. There is such a fine line there. On one hand, to say bullying has never been a factor in some of these cases would be foolishness. Yet, on the other hand, to say a person who was doing the bullying is totally responsible for the actions of another person is an overreaction, just as out of balance.

We must stop the insanity, for both are giving too much power to the aggressor. We must create an environment where it's okay to talk about bullying and abuse, to know it's okay to break the silence, because no one deserves that kind of treatment for any reason.

To be a silent victim or bystander is not the answer. Yet, if we say anyone who has been hurt has the right to hurt another, it's only going to get worse. Do you see what I mean? This system is a monster and it wants control.

I found I couldn't stand up against society's system on my own. I felt helpless when left to my own power. It was controlling me. Just as the first steps in the 12 steps of Alcoholics Anonymous are to admit being powerless over addiction and needing to find a higher power to restore sanity, we need to do the same thing to restore sanity in our world.

Likewise, I believe the first step to being free from society's system is to admit it's controlling us. Whatever or whoever is master over you is your boss or king. This system is the kingdom of this society. The philosophy of this kingdom is to live for No. 1. Selfishness is its religion and its trinity is Me, Myself and I. "Me-ism" is its motto, and its mission is to gratify *My* desires at anyone's expense while attempting to appear a little better than the next guy. The problem is, you're never satisfied, for the system is always trying to convince you that you just need a little more.

Be honest, do you, like me, feel you're on the treadmill of life going nowhere but you can't shut it down or get off? You keep yearning for more. You try harder, go faster and become busier, only to feel you have more on your plate than you can handle. How do you stay ahead of the competition? Life becomes something to be conquered rather than enjoyed.

People become commodities used to reach end goals or, if they get in the way, liabilities, leaving many forgotten as casualties of a cultural war. Soon, relationships are forfeited for profit and friendships are lost in the quest for power. Integrity is ignored for image. Family takes a backseat to the career and getting ahead. Families opt for more things or bigger houses, and fewer children. Children are seen as inconveniences, and gadgets as necessities. Commitment is viewed as overrated and a thing of the past. Pleasure, self-fulfillment and progress are pursued at any price. Character is forgotten while importance is placed on plastic surgery and a plastic smile.

It's controlling us.

It doesn't take a lot of intelligence to see people are different: men and women, young and old, black, white, red, yellow and many shades in between. Our physical features are as diverse as the cultures from which we come. There are over seven billion people on this planet. Not only does each of us look different, but each person also has a unique personality with likes and dislikes. Too often, our differences have caused division instead of appreciation and unity. Our history books are filled with examples of racial discrimination and segregation, from apartheid to genocide.

I think we like to believe our society is more tolerant, more inclusive and, for lack of a better term, *better* than the societies and generations before us. In many ways, I believe we have made great strides. Unfortunately, we have not yet rid ourselves of prejudice and division.

In most schools, we categorize people as brains, jocks, preppies, nerds, geeks, skaters, druggies and so on. If someone doesn't fit into one of these groups, he or she often falls through the cracks. After high school, there are yet more categories: unskilled labor, housewives, management, welfare recipients, executives, working class, freeloaders, etc. We classify everyone, from the beggar on the street to the entrepreneur who owns half of Wall Street. As a result, we've lost sight of the overall picture. We do not dream of unity, harmony, peace and love, much less experience them in reality.

Our judging and classifications have encouraged feelings of superiority in some and inferiority in most. The weak, hurting, old, minorities and handicapped often feel forgotten. Instead of loving and giving, we are fighting and taking. The strongest dominate our society, and we deteriorate to following the laws of nature or the environment, "survival of the fittest."

I saw a cartoon called "Mountain of Success." At the bottom of a mountain, a woman started climbing. She was perspiring and puffing as she inched toward the top. The crowded path was rough and steep. She stepped on people and pulled others down because she thought it was the only way to make it to the top. When she got to the top her look of accomplishment quickly faded as she looked around. There was another person at the top so she asked, "What's up here, anyway?" The person answered as he pointed to the masses struggling up the hill, "Nothing, but don't tell them."

I want to tell them. I want to scream for all to hear, "That's not where life is found. Life is not a game where the person with the most toys wins." I am not saying we should give up aspirations of success and progress, but we need to find significance and meaning in who we are, not in what we attain.

The system is controlling us. Is there a way to be free? Is there a way to start a Dignity Revolution?

Yes! When you suggest living by a different system where everyone is valued, feels significant and knows their intrinsic worth, many will likely call you a dreamer, idealist or young and naïve. Every person has intrinsic worth that should be valued and celebrated.

Even when exposed, the world's value system can control us to the core of our being because we are so afraid of feeling insignificant, invisible, unimportant or worthless. Perhaps you've tried to stand up against the system, but have felt all alone, or haven't received the encouragement and reinforcement you needed to keep the vision alive. Having failed, you now not only feel worthless, but helpless to change the system or be the person you long to be, to be free. Hope starts to fade and you give up on an idea of a better world and numb your desires.

So, you give in to one of three options:

You give in to the chains of addiction and abuse. You believe the lies you're told that say you don't matter, you're not loved and you can't make a difference. You become fatalistic and throw your life away through unhealthy choices and end up in the landfill of regret, or worse yet, you totally give up on life itself.

If you can't beat 'em, join 'em. In the name of reality, you admit it's a dog-eat-dog world. You give up the ghost and become part of the walking dead. Life loses its luster and becomes one of humdrum survival. You don't live, you exist. You settle. You quit hoping and dreaming.

You look to be just one person up on the food chain. You pretend life is satisfying and you play the game, giving the impression you're in control and everything is okay. "But don't be fooled by me." You keep going through the motions, wearing the masks and building walls. You play the role others expect of you and become an actor in the play of life, never discovering who you are meant to be. You work the system. It's just the way life is. You make the most of it. You only live once, so give it all you've got. Get all you can. Be bigger, go faster, get more, move up, advance, get promoted, earn a raise, fill your calendar, be noticed. Make yourself irreplaceable. Look younger. Live for the now. Entitlement and an "I-deserve-it" attitude become a way of life. You live by the motto, "whatever makes *Me* happy."

Could there be more to life than these three options?

CHAPTER 8

DIGNITY REVOLUTION

Yes! There has to be more to this life than just living and dying. I can't accept there are only a select few who are tall enough, thin enough, pretty enough, successful enough or strong enough to have a healthy identity. We need a foundation where everyone knows they matter, are loved and have dignity, no matter where they fall on the bell chart, whether they're from the gifted, handicapped or "normal" segment of society. People need to know there is purpose and meaning to life, that hope and destiny are not just for the movies and fairy tales. They need to believe, to know there can be a bright future and that there is something worth living for, even through the hard times of life.

The answer is so big, so profound, so amazing, even the most intelligent people in the world have only begun to scratch the surface. They continue to grasp and try to understand the reality of this marvelous truth. All the books of the world cannot capture it. It stumps academia. We cannot fully comprehend this mysterious and profound truth, realizing there is always more to be learned.

Yet, at the same time, it's a message so profoundly simple that its essence can be understood by a child. For you see, if we do not have a message that can touch every person in every nation, in any language, sex or religion, then I believe the message is not a universal truth. The message cannot be for only the intellectually elite. This Dignity Revolution should be available for all—every child, boy, girl, man, woman, young, old, rich or poor … liberty and justice for all.

Do you want it? Do you believe it? Do you see what could be? Can you taste the hope this would bring? Can you envision how this could change the world one person at a time?

The message is this: Every person has dignity. This revolution centered on people's dignity could really happen. Please don't give into the false impression that we're too far gone. To have it become a reality means it has to start with me … you … right here … right now.

We can create a movement where we say enough is enough. Starting today, you can say, "I will stand up for people and stand against society's system for determining self-worth. I refuse to live by society's values that demean people. I will speak up for those who can't speak for themselves. I will not be silent about this system that is not working. With everything in me, I will rebel against any system that is unfair and treats others as less than human. I will break free from the control it has on me."

History has shown how people have hoped for a new way of life, such as through political revolution. The people catch a vision and strive to break free, but don't have the power to overthrow the reigning government, ruler, dictator or powers that be. Governments have been toppled in hopes of something better, only to be replaced by anarchy and a life worse than before.

Let's look at the power we really need, and how we can get it and implement a new system.

Not only do we need to rebel against the old system, we need to provide a better way—a *real* Dignity Revolution. We need to change the old system and establish a new one. We must understand this is not a political revolution or new government, nor is it a campaign against capitalism or a socioeconomic revolution. Honestly, it's bigger. This has more hope, more opportunity for lasting change.

It's a Dignity Revolution—a heart revolution, a thoughts-and-values revolution. It's a matter of the heart that can impact the very fabric of society and how we treat people, how we view others and ourselves. It's new because it's giving us the power to stand up against the old system and not allow it to form our identity, or guide our thoughts, feelings and actions. We cannot let the bully win, rule and dictate. We can choose to no longer allow the old system to control us.

This movement is so simple a child can comprehend and live by it, yet it's so brilliant it cannot be bottled by the academic world.

It's time for action. It's time to fight, not with guns or military, not with bombs or hatred, but with the only weapon that can change the hearts of people and the world.

I turn again to my special needs sister, Lois. So many experiences with Lois have shaped my life, from my questions of why she is different than others to why she had to be born into my family. My experiences have ranged from being embarrassed by her at times to pretending not to know her, to wanting to defend her and hurt those who have hurt her.

Lois has been, and is, a teacher to me. She has shown me what life is all about. Lois never lets the "bell" dictate her value or dignity. She has found freedom from society's system. She has toppled the system's reign in her life. I want what she has so badly, and I want every person I know to live by this truth and share it with others.

Lois lives her life on a foundation that cannot be shaken. What is this weapon that can topple powers and grant us a new system by which to live? What is the foundation? There's one more component to the bell I drew earlier …

… Love. Yes, love!

That's it? Really, Bob? That's the great and profound culmination of this book? Seriously?

Is that what you're thinking? Before you roll your eyes and laugh, re-calling romantic comedies, or write me off as a cheesy or dreamy idealist, or shake your head believing I do not understand the complexities of life, intensity of the problems or depth of the pain, please hear me out.

We have lost the understanding of love. Our definition of love now can range from loving a new iPhone or haircut to loving our nation and dying to defend it.

The ancient Greeks had a deeper understanding of the many types of love and used different terms to describe it: *philia*/friendship; *storge*/family; *eros*/romance.

But the Greeks had one more word for love, greater than all of the previous three combined. It's called *agape* love, an unconditional love that accepts us just the way we are, no strings attached. Agape love is selfless, building others up, expecting nothing in return. It is *true* love.

A story about Lois perfectly demonstrates this agape love. My mom worked with a 24-hour hotline. People who were struggling or had problems would call, and Mom would try to give advice or put them in touch with an agency to help them.

One night she received a call, and Lois happened to be sitting in the room as my mom spoke on the phone. The conversation Lois overheard went something like this: "What? He lost his job? They overthrew the union? No unemployment? No, really? They have how many children? Four? And welfare can't help until when? Oh, that's terrible."

When Lois heard this she began to cry, big crocodile tears rolling down her cheeks. "It's not fair that they don't have any money," she said. Then her demeanor suddenly changed. She actually became excited. She jumped up from her chair and waved her arms. She began "snort-ing," as though she were half laughing and half crying. This was such a common occurrence at our house that, whenever she did it, we would simply say, "There goes Lois again."

Lois ran to her bedroom and grabbed an envelope from her dress-er drawer and ran back to my mom. With tears still streaming down her face, but excitement in her eyes, she said, "Here, Mom, give this to them. This will feed them for a long time."

My mom, still on the phone, smiled and reached for the envelope. She opened it and her eyes filled with tears, too. What was inside?

Lois works in a special program assembling parts for a company that provides job-training opportunities for those who are disabled or handicapped. Inside the envelope was her paycheck for an entire week's wages, 40 hours of her life. The amount of the check may surprise you. It was for $1.19. Why? Because Lois is paid based on another external, yet another "P" called "piece count," where her pay is based on her output or performance.

Lois had such a compassionate heart that she was willing to give an entire week's pay to help children she didn't know buy food they

SELF-ACTUALIZATION
Pursue Inner Talent | Creativity | Fulfillment

SELF-ESTEEM
Achievement | Mastery | Recognition | Respect

BELONGING-LOVE
Friends | Family | Spouse | Lover

SAFETY
Security | Stability | Freedom from Fear

PHYSIOLOGICAL
Food | Water | Shelter | Warmth

Abraham H. Maslow's Hierarchy of Needs[1]

needed. She was willing to give all she had, not even enough to buy a Big Mac® with a coupon, but she gave what she had, 40 hours of her life, agape love, unconditional and selfless. She loved; true love.

Society's system wants to tell her she's not gifted or valuable. Again, I ask, "Would you tell her?" Lois believes she is beautiful, gifted and valuable. She is proud of who she is. Would you tell her otherwise?

If you're not willing to tell Lois that she isn't valuable, then maybe it's time to learn some life lessons from her. Some people may be too proud to admit someone like Lois could teach them anything. What would that say about them, or how they value her and her contribution to society, or the value and contribution of anyone who may be different?

The lesson is this: The meaning of life, our purpose itself, is found in love. The old system says only one person can be the best, but the new system says everyone can be their best, and every person has meaning, worth and purpose.

It seems so simple, yet is so profound we miss it. In it, we find the power to resist the old and establish the new system—love. I believe it's what we should focus on, and I believe it's what our heart longs for. I believe love should be our aim, vision and goal in life. When we focus on our individuality, we lose love, but when we focus on love, we will find new freedom in our individuality. This is not just my opinion or a starry-eyed philosophy. Even the most educated and scientific scholars like Abraham Maslow agree—we *need* love (see chart above).

We have physical needs, yes, but we need an encompassing love like we need oxygen, water, food and shelter.

People can disagree about how these needs can be filled or met, but I suspect we can at least agree that we all have them.

As humans we have so much in common. I've spoken in 19 countries including India, Tanzania, the Philippines, Thailand, Honduras and Finland. We all laugh, have hopes, experience disappointments, have customs and traditions, and we all bleed red. At the heart, we are the same. We should see people as people, all needing love and a purpose.

I saw a T-shirt that read, "Love sees no colors." At first I thought *how cool.* But as I pondered the statement, I thought *why can't love see colors? Is love dumb? Is love really blind?* The problem isn't the different colors. The problem is when one color is chosen or treated better than another.

I believe love *should* see and embrace the colors. Love *should* recognize the differences and learn from them. Love *should* celebrate the differences in people and cultures. Think how boring the world would be if we were all the same. Equality is not sameness. We are all different, yet equal. We are equal, yet so awesomely unique.

We've wanted to be significant so badly that we've been living for No. 1, for ourselves. Yet, when we live a selfish lifestyle, there's no real lasting joy, no purpose or meaning to life. So many have bought into "I just need to do what makes me happy," even when it's not the loving choice or is at the expense of someone else's dignity.

When we live for and by love, and stand up for the dignity of every person, it brings purpose to our hearts and lives. We were never meant to live life alone. We were designed to live in healthy relationships with others. We've been designed for love.

I know it sounds like I have my head in the clouds. Maybe we need to bring these ideas to Earth and live them out. We are all longing for more. I'm here to tell you, "This is it … love." You may have been hurt before and are afraid of being hurt again, but I believe perfect love will overcome fear.

There are familiar words recited at almost every wedding I've ever been to that share what love is. I suspect you've heard them, too. I think they show what we really long for and need, whether physically, emotionally, socially or spiritually. The verses come from a letter written in the first century to the people of Corinth, a city in the Roman Empire:

> *Love is patient, love is kind and is not jealous;*
> > *love does not brag and is not arrogant,*
> *does not act unbecomingly; it does not seek its own, is not provoked,*
> > *does not take into account a wrong suffered,*
> *does not rejoice in unrighteousness, but rejoices with the truth;*
> *bears all things, believes all things, hopes all things,*
> > *endures all things.*
> *Love never fails;*
> *But now faith, hope, love, abide these three;*
> > *but the greatest of these is love.*[2]

Love is the answer. It is the only thing that can fuel this Dignity Revolution. How can we know what love is and apply it to our own world? Take these same words and substitute your name for the word *love* …

> _____ *is patient, love is kind and is not jealous;*
> > _____ *does not brag and is not arrogant,*
> *does not act unbecomingly; it does not seek its own, is not provoked,*
> > *does not take into account a wrong suffered,*
> *does not rejoice in unrighteousness, but rejoices with the truth;*
> *bears all things, believes all things, hopes all things,*
> > *endures all things.*
> _____ *never fails;*
> *But now faith, hope, love, abide these three;*
> > *but the greatest of these is love.*

How did you feel as you wrote your name? What did you learn?

I try to live up to agape love every moment of my life, and I've resolved to spend the rest of my life pursuing it. This goal of agape love is almost like a cosmic reality—something so much bigger than ourselves, yet it's the very thing to provide the power we need to reach our goal.

Can you imagine a world where everyone embraced the true meaning of love and lived out the qualities listed in the verses above? Maybe it's difficult to imagine the world living out these qualities, let alone your city, school or family. But what about you? You and only you are responsible for the choices you make. Will you choose to love? Will you choose to truly live out these qualities? It will radically change your life and radically impact the lives of those around you.

May we never believe that anyone, from Lois to the most gifted or talented, to the socially awkward, to those in between, should ever be treated as if they are not worthy of life. Instead, my hope is for all of us to believe and live out the truth that every person, including you, has worth and is worthy of life.

Will you pursue love with all that is in you? Will you join together with others and commit that every person is worth loving? Will you commit to a new and better world? Will you join me and become part of the Dignity Revolution?

CHAPTER 9

LIFE LESSONS FROM LOIS

You may still be asking, "But what does this Dignity Revolution really mean for me?" Perhaps the best way to sum it up is to ask you to live like Lois. I believe if the following lessons are lived out, they will be the driving force behind a Dignity Revolution. If everyone practiced these lessons, it could be the end of the bullying and emotional abuse experienced in today's society. Even if it is not possible to stop all bullying, love can still win.

The goal and the motivation for the Dignity Revolution is really love, so these 25 life lessons could also be called love lessons.

1 Lois accepts people for who they are.

2 Lois always tells the truth.

3 Lois always stands up and challenges the aggressor if someone is being hurt or put down.

4 Lois is assertive and always does her best. She takes a healthy pride in her accomplishments, such as participation in Special Olympics (*SpecialOlympics.org*).

5 Lois isn't ashamed when she is not able to do something on her own. She is willing to accept assistance.

6 Lois knows she is a valuable person, no matter what.

7 Lois isn't afraid to show her emotions.

8 Lois tells someone in authority if something is wrong and seeks help.

9 Lois isn't afraid to sing loud, even though she may not know all the words. And she dances when there's music, whether she's alone or if people are watching.

10 Lois is always there with a smile or a needed hug.

11 Lois knows life is better when lived with friends and family.

12 Lois knows life has more meaning when you help others. That's why she volunteers in the Sunday school class for infants.

13 Lois knows the benefits of forgiveness … forgiving others, asking forgiveness, forgiving herself.

14 Lois knows the joy of giving, having given her hard-earned money to help the poor.

15 Lois doesn't judge people based on the color of their skin, the clothes they wear, the money they have or their athletic abilities.

16 Lois would never speak evil about anyone or humiliate them. She doesn't even like it when I refer to someone as "spoiled rotten." I have to say "spoiled good."

17 Lois works hard, plays hard and knows how to simply sit in a swing and enjoy the breeze. She has a balanced life.

18 Lois knows the significance of making a difference and having a cause she cares about. She saves the pull-tabs from soda cans for Ronald McDonald House Charities.®

WHATEVER THIS LIFE BRINGS, ALL OF US DESERVE TO FEEL VALUED.

19 Lois is willing to receive advice. My dad always said, "Wear a hat when fishing to block the sun," and my mom always said, "Eat your vegetables." Lois wisely does both.

20 Lois has a sense of modesty. She has often said to me, "Shhh, Bob, I can't talk to you about that. It's a girl thing."

21 Lois prays when she's thankful, prays when she's sad, prays when she loses things and prays for others.

22 Lois always listens to both sides and does not let differences cause separation.

23 Lois has learned to take timeouts, that anger in itself isn't wrong, but she doesn't let it take control.

24 Lois does not say hurtful or bad words, not even *shut up*. She'd respond, "Hey, that's not nice."

25 Lois lives out love and respect to all.

It's my hope you will partner with me in creating a system that declares the value and worth of every human being.

Our Dignity Revolution begins by creating a world where life has purpose and meaning for all, including you and me. It doesn't matter what people have done to us or what mistakes we have made in the past. Whatever this life brings, all of us deserve to feel valued.

As part of the Dignity Revolution, you can choose to be part of the solution instead of part of the problem, and commit to creating a new system where all people are loved, valued and respected.

Are you ready? If so, then it's time to put your newfound determination to make a difference into action. In the following chapter you will find ways to do just that, along with valuable supportive materials and resources that can empower you with the knowledge and lifeskills you need to demonstrate your new commitment and resolve.

Will you be a part of the Dignity Revolution and invite others to join you? It starts with you. It starts here.

Pledge to begin today.

DIGNITY REVOLUTION PLEDGE

I want to be a part of the Dignity Revolution, a movement that stands up for the value of every person, one that stands against society's system for determining self-worth and what society says I have to be, have, or do to feel good about myself.

I choose to stand up against mistreatment of, or injustice toward, any individual or any group of people.

I declare that no one, for any reason, deserves to be demeaned or bullied.

I pledge and commit …

1 • To always be kind, friendly, humane, compassionate and thoughtful of others.
• To be considerate of the needs of others and never be harsh, cruel or mean.
• To "do unto others as I would have them do unto me," and to live by this Golden Rule.

2 • To always be loving, for love is not an emotion, but a decision.
• To do what's best for all involved.
• To hold the feelings, property, being and reputation of others in high regard.
• To be caring and not hurt, harm or hate anyone.

3 • To be a person of peace, that as far as it depends on me, I will be at peace with everyone.
• To work toward unity and harmony, where all is in order.
• To promote reconciliation.
• To agree to disagree.
• To not let differences or disagreements lead to hostility or belittlement.

4 • To be a person of patience.
• To live a life of empathy.
• To try to understand where someone is coming from.
• To have the willpower to stay the course when things get difficult.
• To not give in to frustration and allow anger to control choices.

5 • To be a person of goodness.
• To be an authentic person.
• To be an example to others in areas of integrity.
• To be fair, just and courteous to others in all I say and do.
• To live by the truth that life isn't measured by what is received, but by what is given.
• To give from a heart of generosity and volunteerism.

6 • To always bring true joy everywhere, while sincerely acknowledging the sorrow, sadness and brokenness in the world.

• To be a pleasure to those around me.

• To offer a smile of encouragement and a shoulder of comfort.

• To keep a good sense of humor and use it to cheer and build people up.

• To bring hope everywhere.

7 • To be a person of faithfulness.

• To be trustworthy.

• To be reliable, someone who can be counted on.

• To be a person of my word—do what I say and say what I mean.

• To be a person of principle.

• To never be disloyal, dishonorable or spread gossip.

• To never use words—spoken, written or in the cyberworld—to malign someone's reputation.

8 • To be a person of gentleness.

• To be a person who is careful with words and actions, demonstrating true meekness, which is not a weakness, but a strength.

• To not be arrogant or feel superior to anyone else.

• To be a person of true humility.

• To be a person of passion and ambition, but never at the expense of another's value or dignity.

• To not put others down in an effort to boost my own self-esteem.

• To stand firm against intolerance, but never at the cost of cruelty, for mercy always triumphs over judgment.

9 • To be a person of self-control in society, whatever life brings.

• To be resilient and never let pain, the past or problems take away choices.

• To be a person of discipline and dignity.

• To be strong in the storms of life and a person of character.

• To be in control of choices by never giving in to insecurities, rage or vices.

10 • To be a friend to all.

• To never be a silent bystander when wrong is being done.

• To tell someone when injustice happens, and stand up for what's right.

• To celebrate differences.

• To not tolerate unacceptable behavior or treatment of others.

• To stand for human decency.

• To show respect to everyone.

• To let every person know they matter through my actions and words.

I pledge to be a part of the Dignity Revolution.

_____
Name   *Date*

_____
Witness   *Date*

As a demonstration of your pledge, download the free Dignity Revolution pledge card and keep it with you as a reminder of the values you have committed to uphold.

Visit *DignityRevolutionPledge.com.*

Front

Back

I pledge to uphold the worth, value and dignity of others, and commit to be a part of the *Dignity Revolution*.

Signature

FOR STUDENTS: THE ABCs OF THE DIGNITY REVOLUTION: 21-DAY CHALLENGE

f this Dignity Revolution is to be more than just a book, if it is to become a way of life, then finishing the book is just the beginning, not the end.

This new love system, "way of life," is a decision you make, a pledge you take. It also requires changing bad habits of the old system and forming new habits and behaviors.

To accomplish this takes new thinking and reprogramming of patterns and beliefs. It will take work to dispel statements of those who have said, "You're not good enough. You don't matter. You'll never measure up." Some of us have believed those statements for so long that we feel chained to them, unable to break free or change. You can become the person you long to be, a person who values all people, including yourself.

I wish I could say it was easy as ABC, but it's hard. It will be a process. But it's said practice makes perfect, so to reinforce the truth of this book, I came up with some ABCs to help.

We need to go back to the basics until they become the new normal, until we believe in them to our core. A lot of these ABCs are common sense, but I've also heard it said that common sense isn't so common anymore.

HERE'S HOW THE ABCs WORK:

DAY 1 For the next 21 days, read through the ABCs. Make these truths part of your routine until they become habit.

DAY 2 Each day, select in order the listed behavior you need to embrace and DO IT. Make this behavior part of you, part of your day, part of your life, and reflect it in your actions. Make a note of this behavior and carry it with you as a reminder of your commitment to the Dignity Revolution.

DAY 3 With each behavior, ask yourself, "How can I … ?" Example: Day 1, "How can I … accept unconditional love?" Because you are loved for who you are, not for what you do.

Perhaps the first day's question will challenge you to receive a gift or help from someone and not feel like you needed to earn it or return the favor.

For me, I often struggle with the second day's challenge: accepting a compliment. I make fun of myself a lot. It's important to know it's okay to laugh at yourself. But when someone offers me a compliment,

I usually make a joke and deflect the affirmation instead of accepting it. I use my humor as a shield. I need to continually remind myself to simply offer a thank-you and believe it. I'm getting a little better. Still, I'm realizing I might have to take my own advice and practice the ABCs again … and again.

Share the ABCs with others. Share this book. But more importantly, share your heart. Share love. Let's begin living the Dignity Revolution.

Remember, a new habit or behavior might feel awkward at first, but with repetition it will begin to feel natural. The Dignity Revolution depends on courage, compassion, commitment and consistency, one day at a time.

"Be the change you wish to see in the world," *Mahatma Gandhi*

THE ABCs OF CREATING A NEW SYSTEM

ACCEPT …

DAY 1 Unconditional love. You are loved because of who you are, not what you do.

DAY 2 Compliments and affirmation. Look someone in the eye when you receive a compliment, and allow friends you trust to see behind the masks.

DAY 3 That development of a solid identity is a process, and know that it takes time to truly change and grow.

DAY 4 Rejection as part of life. Allow hard times to build character and serve as an opportunity to grow and learn.

DAY 5 Weaknesses. You won't be good at everything and you will fail, but take healthy risks and learn to laugh at yourself.

DAY 6 Others. Love others the way you want to be loved.

BELIEVE …

DAY 7 That love wins.

DAY 8 That you are valuable. Not only are you unique, but you are awesomely created.

DAY 9 In the power of forgiveness. Forgive others and yourself.

DAY 10 There is a purpose for life, that you can make a difference and impact those around you.

DAY 11 That different is not wrong.

CHOOSE …

DAY 12 To use the love system. Look for opportunities to focus on and affirm internal qualities.

DAY 13 To do what is right, even at the cost of acceptance.

DAY 14 To listen to music, read books, and watch movies and TV that are consistent with your values.

DAY 15 To give of your time and talents to help others.

DAY 16 To promote life by loving and accepting all people.

DAY 17 To acknowledge issues and feelings instead of avoiding them.

DECLARE …

DAY 18 The power of love. Set an example by what you say and do.

DAY 19 The dignity of every human life. Stand against social, racial and sexual injustice.

DAY 20 Your feelings, and find healthy ways to be heard.

DAY 21 Faith, hope and love always, for those qualities are lasting.

FOR STUDENTS: LIFESKILLS MAKE THE DIFFERENCE

Lifeskills are abilities that help develop the capacity to engage in positive behaviors and nurture our well-being and the well-being of others.

These skills help us to critically think so we can become effective problem-solvers. Lifeskills also help us choose positive behaviors that enable us to deal effectively with the demands and challenges of everyday life.

Learning and practicing lifeskills, such as decision-making processes and effective interpersonal communication, can reinforce and affirm qualities of self-worth and resiliency to help us take action and generate positive change—a Dignity Revolution.

We identified earlier in the book that society's system is not working, is not fair, is dehumanizing and is controlling us. Therefore, in order to have a Dignity Revolution, we need to respectfully stand up for what is right. In order to do this, the five essential lifeskills listed below are vital to respectfully changing a system that is not working.

1. MAKING TOUGH DECISIONS

There are situations in this book where critical decisions had to be made, where the outcome of those decisions could either hurt or help another person. For instance, in Chapter 3, following football practice when Bob saw some of his teammates gang up on Jack and hang him on the fence, it was at this moment when Bob had to make a decision. He had to decide whether to help Jack off of the fence or leave him there, hanging helplessly, and laugh at him along with the other guys on the football team.

When trying to make a healthy decision we have to critically weigh the positive and negative options, consider all the alternatives and try to forecast the outcome of each option to determine the best choice for that particular situation.

As part of the Dignity Revolution, we need to make healthy decisions that are respectful, value others and sustain dignity for every person. There are two decision-making models that can be used.

The first is called "The Quick 5." To use this lifeskill, you need to ask yourself the following five questions:

*Is it **safe**?*
*Is it **healthy** (emotionally, physically, socially, etc.)?*
*Is it **legal**?*
*Is it **respectful** (to myself, others and the community)?*
*Is it in line with my **values** (and the values of my friends and family)?*

As an example, here are some ways Bob could have applied "The Quick 5" to his situation with Jack:

*Is it **safe**? Is Jack in danger?*
*Is it **healthy**? Will Jack experience emotional turmoil or social rejection?*
*Is it **legal**? Could I get in trouble with the law?*
*Is it **respectful**? Is Jack being respected? Is the team?*
*Is it in line with my **values**? Will my response make me and/or my family proud?*

If the answers to "The Quick 5" are all *yes*, then the decision you are about to make is probably a healthy decision. If the answer is *no* to any of the five questions, the decision you are about to make is probably an unhealthy one and will most likely have negative consequences for you or someone else.

In the other decision-making model, we critically think through all the possible consequences, positive and negative, pertaining to making a decision. This lifeskill, "The Big 6," asks us to explore the risks associated with each option as it guides us into making a healthy choice that can help resolve our situation.

STEP 1 *Define the problem or decision you need to make.*
• Be specific regarding the reason for making a decision.
• Identify what your own feelings and reactions might be to the present problem.

STEP 2 *List your possible options or choices.*
• Develop at least three possible and realistic choices or options you might have regarding this problem.

STEP 3 *List the consequences, positive and negative, for each option or choice in Step 2.*
• Brainstorm all the negative outcomes for each possible option or choice.
• Brainstorm all the positive outcomes for each possible option or choice.

STEP 4 *Refer to "The Quick 5."*
• Select the best option based on the negative and positive options you listed in Step 3.
• Ask yourself if this option is safe, legal, healthy, respectful of self and others, and does this option follow your/your family's guidelines and values. If *yes* to all five questions …

STEP 5 *Make a decision.*
• Choose the best option.
• Act on this option.

STEP 6 *Evaluate your decision.*
• Was the problem resolved?
• Did the decision meet your needs and/or the needs of others?
• If not, go through the process again and select another option.

No one is born with awesome decision-making skills. Decision-making is a lifeskill that needs to be learned and strengthened throughout our lives. A trusted and respected friend or mentor can be a great help to walk through these skills with you. They can often bring a fresh perspective and lovingly help you recognize things about yourself you may not see. Whether on your own or with a trusted friend, the more you practice making healthy decisions by using the "The Quick 5" or "The Big 6," the better you will be at it. And the better we are at making healthy decisions, the better our world will be.

Another way to help you learn these skills is to complete "The Big 6" worksheet included in this book (Appendix B). It will help you, step by step, answer these questions and consider the options. It's a great and practical exercise to go through as you evaluate your responses to various situations in life.

2. LET'S TALK: EFFECTIVE COMMUNICATION

How we communicate with each other encompasses a variety of strategies and techniques critical to our Dignity Revolution. Using effective communication skills is not a matter of just being "nice." Rather, it helps us share our true selves with other people and it gifts us with a genuine sense of understanding at a deeper level. When we communicate effectively, conflict is more likely to be resolved rather than escalate, and relationships are more likely to be built than destroyed. Communicating well gives dignity and respect to both the sender and the receiver of a conversation.

One of the essential elements of effective communication is the use of "I" messages. "I" messages are a way of saying how you feel without blaming or attacking anyone. "I" messages help to de-escalate conflict and they can prevent us from saying something we might later regret. "You" messages, on the other hand, tend to evoke defensiveness and escalate emotions rather than solve a problem.

There are two "I" message communication skills you can use to interconnect more effectively. One is called the "I" Formula Skill and the other is called the Carefrontation Skill.

The "I" Formula Skill would typically be used to share with someone how you feel about an immediate situation or behavior.

"I" Formula Communication Skill

HAPPY   AFRAID   SAD   ANXIOUS   HURT   CONFUSED

I feel … (State a feeling/emotion.)

When you … (Explain what they were doing.)

Because … (How their behavior impacted you.)

And I need you to/Would you consider … (What would you like/
    want/need the other person to do/think about? Or, perhaps,
    it is here where you suggest a solution to resolve the issue.)

For example, when Sammy prevented Lois from riding her trike on the sidewalk and Sammy's behavior made Bob really mad, Bob might have said: *"I felt really angry when you didn't allow my sister to ride her trike on the sidewalk because she enjoys it and has the right to ride her trike on the sidewalk. I would like you to allow her to do this."*

Oftentimes, people we care about who use drugs, bully others or choose unhealthy behaviors don't see the negative effects those behaviors have on them or others. To help those we care about change their destructive behaviors we need to confront them with dignity and love. Using the Carefrontation Skill can provide you with the opportunity for sharing how you feel about their behavior in a loving and nonconfrontational way. But what if they don't change? It's important to know that no one can control another person's actions or feelings. We need to know what our responsibility is. Even if the other person doesn't change, you can't allow them and their behavior to change you in a negative way.

Carefrontation Communication Skill

I care/love you … (It's critical to let the person you are talking to know you are confronting them about their behavior because you care for them.)

I see … (Describe in detail the behavior you are concerned about—
    who, what, where, when, etc.)

I feel … (Share how you feel when this person behaves in this manner.)

Listen … (Give the other person a chance to explain their situation.)

I want/Would you consider … (Explain in detail what you need or
    would like the person to do.)

I will … (Explain in detail what you are going to do to help them
    and/or yourself in the situation.)

In Chapter 3, we discovered Ronny never talked to anyone about the abuse he was experiencing, and for reasons we may never know, Ronny took his own life. Imagine for a minute you had a friend like Ronny who was depressed or you suspected had an eating disorder. How would you share your concerns with them? What might this carefrontation skill look and sound like?

> *Jamie, you are my very best friend and I **love** you. I am talking to you because I **care** about you and I need to tell you what I have been **noticing** during the past two weeks. On Monday, you didn't sit with us during lunch, and for the past two weeks you seem to have isolated yourself from your friends during lunchtime. I noticed your clothes look like they are too big for you and you appear to be losing weight. Yesterday after lunch, I heard you throwing up in the bathroom. I am **feeling** really scared and I am **concerned** you might have an eating disorder. Can you tell me what is going on? (**Listen** to what your friend might have to say.) I **would like you** to consider going with me to the counselor's office so we can talk about this. I **will** go with you today. (Or you could say, "If you do not go to the counseling office with me, because I love you I **need to** let the counselor and/or your parents know what I am seeing.")*

Using this skill, out of love and concern for your friend, might help your friend ask for and/or receive the help they need.

While people have been communicating for centuries without communication skills, people have also been miscommunicating for centuries. Learning a few new lifeskills regarding how we communicate with each other can help us sustain our Dignity Revolution and ultimately build stronger and healthier relationships.

3. LET'S LISTEN

Ever wonder why we have two ears and only one mouth? Perhaps we need to listen twice as much as we speak.

Listening to what a person is sharing with us is a way to respectfully respond and value their thoughts, message and opinions. Listening enables the speaker to find out whether the listener really understood what they had to say. Really paying attention to what another person is telling us enables us to show we value that person and it helps avoid misunderstandings.

Listen with L.O.V.E.

Listen for important facts and feelings.

Observe body language. Look for what the person might not be saying with words, but with actions.

Verify your understanding by asking questions or summarizing.

Empathize by putting yourself in the other person's situation.

Listening makes our loved ones feel worth. Listening with love, lifeskills can fuel our social and emotional success and it is an essential part of the Dignity Revolution.

4. HOW TO APOLOGIZE

We all need to learn how to apologize. After all, no one is perfect and we all make mistakes. In Chapter 4, we talked about how "hurting people hurt people," and that a sincere apology shows you are taking responsibility for your actions. An apology is an acknowledgment and confession that you engaged in unacceptable behavior and want to re-build trust and restore dignity to the person you hurt. It is not always easy to apologize, but it is an effective way to restore balance and trust in a relationship, as well as strengthen your self-confidence and self-respect.

When you make your apology, don't be tempted to explain or justify your actions. This will only sound like an excuse and can weaken your apology. Instead be honest, truthful and sincere with your words. It's never too late to apologize.

I am so sorry for … (Sincerely state what you did and take responsibility for your actions.)

Can you please forgive me?

What can I do to make this right? Or, How can I/we fix it?

Follow through on your promise and amend the hurt.

5. REFUSAL SKILLS

Refusal skills are a set of skills designed to help avoid participating in high-risk and/or unhealthy behaviors. They help us resist peer pressure while maintaining our self-respect and dignity.

Even if you are committed to the Dignity Revolution, others can make it hard for you. The first step is to identify what kind of pressure you might be feeling. It could be a direct pressure where another person tries to persuade you to engage in a behavior that is not in alignment with the Dignity Revolution pledge you signed, or you could be tempted internally to engage in a behavior that does not value or give dignity to yourself or others.

Whenever you feel pressure to do something you do not want to do, think about using a refusal skill from the list below or come up with your own. As you gain confidence in using your refusal skills, it will become easier to confront or avoid a difficult situation. Remember, saying *no* can sometimes be hard, but you might be surprised how easy it becomes with practice.

Ask questions. If someone asks you to do something, question the person to identify if there is potential trouble or a health risk associated with the activity: *Did your parents say this was okay? Do we have permission to be here? Is anyone else showing up?*

Use the "The Quick 5." Ask yourself: *Is what I am being asked to do safe, healthy, legal, respectful, and does it follow my values?*

State the consequence and repeat it. If the pressure for you to do something continues, state a negative consequence that might result if you engage in the activity or behavior and repeat it over and over like a broken record; i.e: *I won't go with you because if I don't take the time to study I will fail my test in algebra and the class.*

Sell an alternative. If the person asks you to engage in a behavior that will get you into trouble, suggest an alternative behavior that is safe, legal, healthy, etc.: *Instead, why don't you come to my house and we can study for the test together.*

Walk away. If the pressure continues for you to do something against your values, tell the person, "No thank you," invite them to come with you to engage in another healthier activity, and then walk away leaving the door open. *Sorry, I am not going to join you, but if you change your mind, let me know.*

Refusing an unhealthy behavior does not necessarily mean you are rejecting the person. It just means you are making a decision that allows you to keep your self-respect, maintain your dignity and confirm your commitment to be part of the Dignity Revolution.

FOR STUDENTS:
BULLYING PREVENTION TIPS

Everyone is different. Every one of us has special gifts and talents that are irreplaceable and essential to the world we live in. We come in a variety of shapes and sizes—short, tall, overweight, underweight—with special needs and wants, and from different cultures. We may look, dress and act differently but, nonetheless, our differences and similarities make our society unique and beautiful.

Unfortunately, in our present system, some people become targets of abuse, bullying or harassment. As part of the Dignity Revolution pledge, we believe people have value and deserve to be respected. We believe people are worthy of dignity and love. We believe no one has the right to purposely hurt another human being and no one should ever have to experience being the target of abuse. Bullying and abusing others through words and actions is harmful. It is hurtful. It is wrong.

Bullying can result in physical injury, social and emotional distress, and even death. Targeted youth are at risk for mental health problems such as depression and anxiety, psychosomatic complaints such as headaches, and poor school adjustment. Youth who bully others are at increased risk for substance use, academic problems and violence later in adolescence and adulthood. Comparing youth who only bully with those who are only targets, victims of bullying suffer the most serious consequences and are at greater risk for both mental health and behavior problems.[1]

In a nationwide survey, 20 percent of high school students reported being bullied on school property in the 12 months preceding the survey.[2]

This has to stop. So what can we do?

In schools where there are antibullying programs, bullying is reduced by 50 percent.[3]

We can raise awareness about bullying and harassment in our schools and communities.

We can start a dialogue with others about their role in addressing bullying and be proactive in stopping it.

We can talk about our differences and support the fact it's okay to be different—no matter what.

We can stop the drama between the target and the bully and teach tolerance, acceptance and kindness.

We can encourage our schools to adopt and participate in harassment, hazing, bullying and abuse prevention policies and programs (see Chapter 11).

Instead of being a bystander, we can be an "upstander," someone who stands up for those who are targets of abuse or those who may not be able to stand up for themselves.

Remember, by doing nothing we are sending a message that it is okay to bully or abuse another human being and that bullying behavior is acceptable.

We need to use our voices against bullying, abuse and violence. We need to step in, speak up and respectfully intervene whenever possible in order to stop the abusive behavior. We *can* help stop the hurt.

We can advocate and spread the word though loving actions and behaviors. We can demonstrate how to value others with dignity and respect. We can practice and use the lifeskills presented in Part Two of this chapter, and we can inspire others and encourage them to join our Dignity Revolution.

A few resources to help you on your journey are:

Centers for Disease Control and Prevention *cdc.gov/violenceprevention*

STRYVE *safeyouth.gov*

Stop Bullying *stopbullying.gov*

U.S. Surgeon General's Report, "Understanding Youth Violence" *surgeongeneral.gov/library/youthviolence*

FOR TEACHERS: EMPOWERING AND ENGAGING STUDENTS

If your plan is for a year, plant rice.
If your plan is for a decade, plant trees.
If our plan is for a lifetime, educate children.
Confucius, adapted

I have the utmost respect for teachers and the challenges they face. I have met thousands of dedicated and impassioned educators through the years who long to not only provide academic knowledge, but lessons on character, value and integrity to guide students through a lifetime.

Teachers play an extremely important role in our society, for it is the teacher who mainly educates the youth of today, who in turn become the leaders of tomorrow. Teachers not only make a positive difference in the lives of children, they *are* a positive difference in the lives of children.

Over the past three decades, researchers and educators have increasingly recognized the importance of the K-12 school climate. Programs, policies and protocol promoting safety and a positive school climate among students should be taught, be in place and easily accessible to parents, staff members and students. Such research-based and user-friendly strategies enable students on campus to feel personal, emotional, behavioral and academic success.

As part of the Dignity Revolution movement, we created the following resources specifically designed for teachers to use with their students and/or within their schools. These tools are meant to assist teachers in starting their very own Dignity Revolution—to use, share and adapt to their specific needs.

The goal of each strategy or policy should be clearly stated so that all members of the school community know that they are expected to respect each other. Respect should govern all interpersonal interactions and attitudes among students, faculty and staff on campus.

Appendix A/Decision-Making: "The Big 6"

Appendix B/*Dignity Revolution* Follow-Up

This section can be used in conjunction with this book to help teachers facilitate personal reflection opportunities for their students. The document also lists suggested group activities teachers can infuse into their classroom curriculum.

Appendix C/Sample Respect Policy

This policy example delineates effective procedures and protocols to help empower students and teachers to create safe and bully-free/harassment-free environments in schools. It helps identify behavioral expectations. Such a policy should be adopted and upheld by students and faculty alike.

Appendix D/Response Protocol for Complaint of Harassment or Bullying

This detailed guideline demonstrates the protocol a staff member or student needs to follow to report and resolve a situation involving harassment or bullying, including suggested questions, responses and next steps.

Appendix E/Sample Bullying/Harassment Report

When a student reports a bullying or harassment incident, use this form to document the situation. One of its key elements, which is different from most referral forms, is that the student, not the teacher, is the one who is asked to complete the report. By asking the student to complete the form, it empowers them to suggest and identify how they would like the incident resolved. Empowering a bystander, the target and even the person who was bullying, puts ownership of the resolution on their shoulders versus the administrator or teacher.

Appendix F/FOR TEACHERS: Top 10 Bullying Prevention Tips

Practical, quick steps are listed to properly address the bully and the target.

Appendix G/FOR PARENTS: Top 10 Bullying Prevention Tips

Oftentimes, parents approach a teacher or administrator seeking guidance on how to help their child who is being bullied or harassed. Working together with a parent to address these issues can be very helpful in combating the problem. Use these tips, along with your encouragement, and inform them of the policies and protocols in place for addressing bullying at school. Suggest they read and learn the lifeskills and activities in which their child is being encouraged to participate. We're never too old to live out the principles and values taught in this book, and never too old to start.

Lifeskills (See Chapter 10: Part 3 for detailed explanation of lifeskills.)

These skills can be infused into a school curriculum to help students develop their capacity to engage in positive behaviors, nurture their own well-being and the well-being of others. In this book, students are encouraged to learn and practice these lifeskills. As a teacher, it is important to grow in your understanding of them and consider infusing them into your existing curriculum. Consider going through them with your students and learning and practicing them together.

Decision-making skills: "The Quick 5" and "The Big 6"
Communication skills: "I" Formula and Carefrontation
Let's listen
How to apologize
Refusal skills

I hope this book will be valuable to you, your classroom and your school. It is my desire to help create a safe atmosphere to cultivate learning with protocols that have been tested and proven. May you feel equipped with the tools you need to empower your students for a lifetime and build them up as individuals who see their value, as well as their potential, in advancing the greater good of all.

I've heard it said love is spelled T-I-M-E. Thank you for loving students. Thank you for your dedication, and for giving part of your life to enrich the lives of others. May the vision for impact and influence that brought you into teaching be renewed and fueled for the great task in front of you.

Teachers play a huge role in this Dignity Revolution. I believe a paycheck was never the reason you came into teaching in the first place, and it's not what keeps you here. Making an impact does. So, may you see hope ignited in the hearts of your students, hope that can only be seen through their eyes, the window to their souls. You have been, are, and will be making a difference.

Together, we can guide a Dignity Revolution.

APPENDIX A | DECISION-MAKING: "THE BIG 6"

NAME OF STUDENT _____ HOUR _____

A decision is the "act of making a choice or coming to a solution." Many decisions involve *risk*, which is a behavior with an element of danger that may cause injury or harm to oneself or others. A person can minimize health risks in a situation when they plan ahead and take precautions. Well-planned, preventive *action* BEFORE an event increases the chances of a safe and healthy outcome.

Think about a situation in your life where you need to make an important decision. Using this worksheet and "The Big 6" decision-making skill, create a healthy solution to your situation.

1. STATE THE SITUATION REQUIRING A DECISION.

THE PROBLEM

2. WHAT ARE THE OPTIONS/CHOICES?

OPTION 1	OPTION 2	OPTION 3

3. LIST ONE POSITIVE AND ONE NEGATIVE CONSEQUENCE FOR EACH CHOICE.

OPTION 1 POSITIVE CONSEQUENCE	OPTION 2 POSITIVE CONSEQUENCE	OPTION 3 POSITIVE CONSEQUENCE
OPTION 1 NEGATIVE CONSEQUENCE	OPTION 2 NEGATIVE CONSEQUENCE	OPTION 3 NEGATIVE CONSEQUENCE

4. ASK YOURSELF "THE QUICK 5."

☐ YES ☐ NO Is it **safe**?
☐ YES ☐ NO Is it **healthy**? *(emotionally, physically, socially, etc.)*
☐ YES ☐ NO Is it **legal**?
☐ YES ☐ NO Is it **respectful**? *(Consider the dignity, value and worth of others and yourself.)*
☐ YES ☐ NO Is it in line with my **values** (and the values of my friends and family)?

5. MAKE A DECISION.

6. EVALUATE YOUR DECISION.

APPENDIX B | *DIGNITY REVOLUTION* FOLLOW-UP

CHAPTER 1 | I DARE YOU

SUMMARY

Bob, the author of *Dignity Revolution*, admits he struggled with insecurities and feelings of inadequacy at times. Yet, he challenges each of us to look beyond our circumstances and become part of a Dignity Revolution.

PERSONAL REFLECTION

… Bob mentions the *ifs* of life—*if* I had money, were better looking, had a different family, etc. What are some of the *ifs* in your life that have made you feel limited in making a difference or living life to the fullest?

… Where and in what areas of your life do you feel insecure?

… Like Bob, are there areas of your life where you may recognize your own arrogance or superiority toward others?

… Who has had the greatest influence on your life? Why?

… What do you feel needs to change in society to help people feel valued and to have dignity?

GROUP ACTIVITY

… Discuss the *ifs* of life that may cause students to feel limited in their ability to make a difference in the world. Explore what students feel hinders them and society from helping everyone feel valued.

… Before reading the following chapters, have students discuss what they feel needs to change in society to help people feel valued and that they have dignity. Record these answers in a place where they can be reviewed later after the students have read the book to see how their answers align with the solutions proposed in this book.

CHAPTER 2 | DON'T BE FOOLED BY ME

SUMMARY

A mask describes a person's ability or tendency to hide their inner characteristics with outer appearances that are not reflective of who they really are. Someone may even wear different masks for different people or situations so they will appear secure and confident, and protect themselves from criticism. We are aware of some masks, and some we are not.

PERSONAL REFLECTION

… How might you be wearing a mask?

… Are there things in life you try to hide from others to protect yourself from criticism?

… What might be examples of masks of which someone may not be aware?

… Do you wear a mask and know it's not working for you, but you keep wearing it anyway? Why?

… Are you feeling more competent, accomplished, accepted and peaceful, or are you in constant fear of being discovered?

… How did reading this chapter create a desire to remove your mask with kindness and understanding, or encourage you to do that for someone else, or both?

GROUP ACTIVITY

… Ask students to write about their mask and how it is used in their life. Ask: "What are you protecting?"

… Ask if anyone is willing to share their written story about their personal masks. This is a journey that students and facilitators need to take together. Give students the opportunity. Do not force anyone to share, yet encourage them. The facilitator should initiate the discussion by first sharing their personal mask.

… Students, if you haven't shared your personal mask with anyone in the discussion group, you are encouraged to find a trusted adult in your life with whom you can share it—counselor, parent, teacher, youth worker, pastor, relative.

CHAPTER 3 | YOU HAVE VALUE

SUMMARY

Bob talks about embarrassment from two perspectives—self-inflicted embarrassment that we bring upon ourselves (when Bob split his pants), and embarrassment caused by someone shaming another person against their will (putting Jack up on the fence post).

PERSONAL REFLECTION

… How has someone intentionally shamed/embarrassed you? How did that make you feel?

… Give an example of how you may have intentionally hurt someone with your action or inaction because you tried to make yourself feel good at someone else's expense?

… Have you witnessed someone being put down at the hands of another person? Did you feel you needed to do something about it and stepped in to defend them, or did you do nothing? How do you feel about your action or inaction? If you did nothing, how did that choice impact you?

… If you stepped in to help, why? What might some of the consequences be for doing the right thing? What are the negative consequences for doing the right thing?

We learned about Bob's friend, Ronny, in Chapter 3. Ronny appeared to have everything he ever wanted—good looks, intelligence, athletic ability, money. Yet, he wore a mask, and inside he felt worthless, unimportant and of no value.

… Have you met Ronnys in life who seem to have it all? How did meeting them make you feel about yourself?

… How did finding out about what really happened in Ronny's life make you feel about the Ronny in your own life? Has it opened your eyes to the possibility that maybe your Ronny isn't as put together as you thought?

… According to culture, society and media, feeling successful and valued requires intelligence, wealth, appearance, abilities, etc. Are they right? Was it true in Ronny's life? Why or why not?

… If society is wrong, what does success and personal value look like to you? What's your definition? What would have made Ronny feel valued?

… The five-dollar bill that Bob abused didn't lose its value. Neither have you. Are you carrying some emotional hurt and pain you need to share? Are you feeling lost and out of control? Have you been abused? If so, I give you permission today to break the silence and talk with an adult who cares—counselor, parent, teacher, youth worker, pastor, relative. Please commit to speaking with someone today.

GROUP ACTIVITY

… Ask students to share a funny, embarrassing moment brought on by themselves. Facilitator, please share one of your own funny, embarrassing moments to help others open up.

… Ask students to share an embarrassing moment brought on by another person that wasn't fun. Facilitator, please share one of your own embarrassing moments to help others open up. How did that experience make you feel?

… Choose two students to participate in a skit. Student No. 1 will approach Student No. 2 and share a plan to play a prank on someone (could include those with special needs; those who are unpopular, overweight, socially awkward; those who don't wear the latest clothes, who are poor, etc.) and humiliate them. Come up with your own scenario, or use an example Bob shared. Student No. 2 can choose to stop the prank by telling someone about it or allow it to happen.

… Instruct Student No. 2 to use the following communication skill: I felt _____ when you _____, because _____ , and I needed _____.

… Discuss both of the characters. What would the consequence be for Student No. 2's choice for the target and themselves if they allowed the prank to continue? What would the consequence be if they stopped it from happening? How would you react if you were Student No. 2?

… Objective: To lead the students to discover why choosing the unpopular thing is often the right thing to do.

… Discuss openly people in popular culture—musicians, actors, pro athletes, leaders, etc.—who appear to have it all, but continually find themselves in trouble, in rehab or even suicidal. What value system do you think is missing that has led to their despair?

CHAPTER 4 | THE SYSTEM ISN'T WORKING
SUMMARY

Many in society go to great lengths to change their outward appearance in a quest to appear physically perfect. Society's system influences us to make extreme decisions to change ourselves leading to plastic surgery, eating disorders, steroid use, etc., to fit a mold of what the world defines as "attractive."

PERSONAL REFLECTION

… What things would you change about your outward identity; i.e., appearance, intelligence, popularity?

… Do you believe changing outward appearances changes the inner sense of peace and belonging?

… If your answer is no, why do you think Americans continue to spend billions of dollars to improve their appearance? When is it okay?

… If your answer is yes, do you think it is working? Is society as a whole feeling a greater sense of belonging—less depression, suicide, and greater self-worth?

… Fill in the blanks in this sentence: "If I could just _____ , then I would feel _____ ."

… Do you think the words you filled in are really true? Would what you wrote really work? Why or why not?

… Do you think the way society's system influences us is wrong and unfair? Why or why not?

… Discussion: Do you believe changing our outward appearance changes our inner sense of peace and belonging?

… If the answer is no, why do people continue to spend billions of dollars on improving their appearance?

… If the answer is yes, then how is it working? Is society as a whole feeling a greater sense of belonging—less depression, suicide, and greater self-worth?

… Discussion: How can we find a balance in properly caring for our appearance without becoming obsessed? What does a healthy balance look like?

… Discussion: What are some of the ways society's system influences us?

CHAPTER 5 | THE SYSTEM ISN'T FAIR
SUMMARY

Chapter 5 begins by discussing the unfairness of the system and the "P's" of society based on external appearances. Bob also introduces his sister, Lois, who has special needs. Yet, Bob shares how he believes she still has value to society.

PERSONAL REFLECTION

… What "P" of society do you feel your friends or peers hold in highest regard?

Physical appearance, what you look like
Performance, how well you do or how successful you are
Possessions, the clothes you wear, the car you drive, the house you own
Popularity, how many friends you have
Pleasure, doing what you want, when you want, because it feels good
Prestige, how recognized or respected you are
Power, how much influence you have over others

… Do you have the same "P" as your friends? If not, what "P" of society do you personally hold in highest regard?

… How are some of your values based on what you have, what you look like and what you can do?

… How do you base the value of others on what they have, what they look like and what they can do?

… Have you experienced a situation of which you were excited to be part only to realize it wasn't meant for you based on what you have, look like or your abilities? How did it make you feel?

… Into which category of the "bell" do you fit—gifted, handicapped or normal? What reasons lead you to believe this? What led you to that diagnosis of yourself?

… "No one deserves to be bullied, harassed, left alone, put down, mocked or made to feel worthless." Do you agree with this statement? Why or why not?

… Do you believe Lois has value? Why or why not? If yes, on what is her value based?

GROUP ACTIVITY

… Anonymously, students write their personal "P" and give to the facilitator.

… Tally all results to identify the most valued "P" of society determined by the group. Post the results, and have a discussion about them.

… How does it make you feel to be part of a group representing this "P" of society?

… Do you believe it is a positive or negative attribute?

… Anonymously, students write into which category of the "bell" they personally feel they fit—gifted, handicapped or normal—and give to the facilitator.

… Tally all results to determine the group outcome. Post the results, and have a discussion about them.

… How does it make you feel to be part of the group?

… Do you believe it is a positive or negative to be in this category?

… What makes a person gifted—looks, intelligence, wealth, etc.?

… How can someone feel valued who doesn't fit society's system for determining worth?

CHAPTER 6 | T4: THE SYSTEM DEHUMANIZES PEOPLE
SUMMARY

This chapter is about one of the most notorious dictators in recent history and his system for determining worth within a society, and how it relates to society today.

PERSONAL REFLECTION

… Hitler identified groups he believed were not valuable to society. Have you been aware of groups of students who have been labeled as persons with little value? Who are they? Who labeled them?

… In what way may you have been mistreated, or how have you mistreated an individual or group of people? How do you feel about it?

… Do you know people in school who are "ringleaders," those who lead/influence others to bully or show disrespect? What does it take to stand up to them? How can you challenge them without bullying them or devaluing them in return?

… Why do you think the majority of people don't stand up to society's system or stand up to bullies?

… What is the deeper longing inside the heart of someone who bullies or puts others down? What is their motivation?

… In an earlier chapter, Bob said "Hurting people hurt people." What does this mean?

GROUP ACTIVITY

… Hitler identified groups he believed were not valuable to society. Identify groups of people in your school; i.e., the handicapped, geeks, popular, jocks, druggies, socially awkward, teachers, etc. Discuss ways these groups may have been devalued by others. Why do you feel they are being bullied, disrespected or devalued?

… Discussion: Why should these various groups not be disrespected or devalued?

… Discussion: How to stand up and challenge someone who is being disrespectful or bullying another person. What skills/resources are necessary to be an empowered bystander?

CHAPTER 7 | WHAT IS CONTROLLING US?
SUMMARY

Bob examines society's system for determining self-worth and challenges our response to those who may hurt us, or others.

PERSONAL REFLECTION

… Bob shared the story of how he defended Lois instead of denying her. What made Bob stand up for her and confront Sammy?

… Bob did the right thing by going to Sammy's mom, but his mom didn't believe Bob. Sometimes when we do the right thing, we may not get the result we hope for. How can we keep standing up?

… Bob wanted to hurt Sammy because he hurt other people. What is an appropriate response?

… How do you keep from responding in anger and becoming the bully yourself?

… Because you have been bullied, mistreated or abused, does it give you a right to do that to another person?

… Is society's system controlling us? List examples of how this system controls your behavior.

… Judging others encourages feelings of superiority. Be honest, do you feel superior to others? Who? How should you treat those with whom you disagree or feel are not as good as you are?

GROUP ACTIVITY

Read the three inappropriate options for managing life's disappointments.

… Give in to addiction and abuse, and believe you don't matter.

… If you can't beat 'em, join 'em.

… Pretend life is satisfying and play the game, giving the impression you are in control and everything is okay.

… Have students individually select and write which of the three they feel describes them personally

…Tally the results and have a discussion around the group's most popular choice.

… Pull questions from the Personal Reflection section above for group discussion.

CHAPTER 8 | DIGNITY REVOLUTION
SUMMARY

Bob identifies what he believes is the solution to overcoming society's system and influence with what some may consider a simplistic answer—love. Yet, he challenges us to live out the example set by his sister, Lois, and find our worth elsewhere.

PERSONAL REFLECTION

… Lois offered her entire paycheck, which was all she had. Have you known of a situation where you wanted to offer something to make it better? If so, explain.

… Bob believes love should celebrate the differences in people. What does that mean to you? Do you agree?

… How can we acknowledge the differences in people and still treat them with equal dignity?

… Do you believe it's okay to do "what makes you happy" even if it hurts other people?

… Can you really be happy if you know your pursuit of happiness is at the expense of someone else and will cause them to be unhappy?

… Would this make you reconsider your actions?

… Knowing what you know now, do you believe happiness is the purpose of life, or that loving others is the purpose of life? Explain.

GROUP ACTIVITY

… Have students write each Greek definition of love.

Phileo/friendship
Storge/family
Eros /romantic
Agape/unconditional

… Have students cite an example, either from their own life or that of someone they know, for each type of love.

… Have students choose one example to share.

… In the book, Bob asks students to substitute their name for the word *love* in the verses quoted. Invite students to review the verses and consider which ones they felt were truthful. Have them complete Appendix H, LOVE: Character Traits.

… Have students consider it their love report card. Ask: "Where can you improve?" Discuss.

CHAPTER 9 | LIFE LESSONS FROM LOIS
SUMMARY

Lois has 25 character traits that exemplify a life lived to the fullest.

PERSONAL REFLECTION

… Bob shares 25 life lessons he learned from Lois. What are the top three that are personal struggles for you? Categorize them as No. 1, No. 2, No. 3. What are you going to do to change the No. 1 struggle?

… What top three life lessons do you feel you are doing well? Categorize them as No. 1, No. 2, No. 3. How can you encourage others to grow in these areas?

GROUP ACTIVITY

… In the Group Activity of Chapter 1 of this *Dignity Revolution* Follow-Up, students recorded comments about what they felt needed to change in society to help people feel valued and to have dignity. Now that they have read the book, review the comments with them to determine how the comments align with the solutions proposed by the author in this book. Have students add to or subtract from the original list.

… Assign each student one of the life lessons and have them share what that life lesson means to them and how they plan on living it out among their peers, family and others with whom they come in contact. Each person who does this ends the sharing with a challenge in their own words; i.e., "Lois accepts people for who they are. I want to challenge each of us to _____."

… Collectively as a class, have students write anonymously the top three life lessons that are struggles for them. Tally the results and identify the top three struggles determined by the class. Discuss ways to improve them among the class and create an action plan.

CHAPTER 10 | DIGNITY REVOLUTION PLEDGE AND SUPPORTING MATERIALS
SUMMARY

These resources will help you to become part of the Dignity Revolution.

… Complete the Dignity Revolution pledge, which can be downloaded from *DignityRevolutionPledge.com*.

… Begin the ABCs' 21-Day Challenge in Part 2.

… Practice "The Quick 5" and "The Big 6." Role-play with a friend in Part 3.

… Practice the lifeskills presented in Part 3.

… Review the bullying prevention tips in Part 4.

APPENDIX C | SAMPLE RESPECT POLICY

Respect is the cornerstone of relationships. We are committed to respecting the dignity and worth of each individual at our school and strive never to degrade or diminish any member of our school community by conduct, actions or attitudes. We benefit from each other. Our diversity makes us strong.

SCHOOL RESPONSE TO BULLYING AND HARASSMENT

Harassment or bullying of students or staff undermines our school's commitment to respect. Bullying and harassment are prohibited by state and federal law, as well as by school policy. Our school will not tolerate bullying or harassment of students or staff.

WHAT IS BULLYING OR HARRASSMENT?		
MAY INCLUDE ANY OF THE FOLLOWING BEHAVIORS	**DIRECTED TOWARD AN INDIVIDUAL BECAUSE OF**	**WHICH CREATES A HOSTILE ENVIRONMENT**
Name-calling	Gender	The behavior is so severe or persuasive that it interferes with an individual's performance or creates an intimidating, hostile or offensive environment.
Making Threats	Race	
Spreading Rumors	Religion	
Telling demeaning jokes	Age	
Making fun of someone	National origin	
Making obscene/provocative gestures	Ancestry	
Physical intimidation	Creed	
Hitting	Pregnancy	
Touching	Marital status	
Pranks and hazing	Sexual orientation	
Vandalism	Physical Traits	
Unwanted pursuit of a relationship	Individual characteristics	
Cyberbullying	Physical or mental disability	
Harassing text messages or calls	Emotional or learning disability	

HOW DO I REPORT BULLYING OR HARASSMENT?

Contact an administrator, counselor, teacher or staff member in person and/or complete the Bullying/Harassment Report (Appendix E) and give it to the appropriate staff member.

Sample respect policy form adapted from that used by North High School, Eau Claire (Wisconsin) Area School District. Compiled by Deborah L. Tackmann and Life Promotions, Inc. Used with permission.

APPENDIX D | RESPONSE PROTOCOL FOR COMPLAINT OF HARASSMENT OR BULLYING

LISTEN, SYMPATHIZE, BUT DON'T JUDGE.

Listen to what the person has to say. Sympathize, but make no judgment or commitment regarding the allegations or how the investigation will be conducted. Do assure the person that your school takes harassment and bullying behavior seriously and will not tolerate it.

PROMPTS

"Tell me what happened."
"Take your time."
"I'm glad you came in."
"Are you comfortable telling me what happened and giving me names?"

TAKE THE REPORT SERIOUSLY.

Assure the person the complaint or problem is being taken seriously and your school will respond to the problem promptly. Avoid using "dangerous words" that minimize the situation and their feelings, such as "It's just teasing, no big deal."

RESPOND TO CONCERNS.

If the person expresses or indicates fear, assure him or her your school will do everything in its power to ensure confidentiality. However, make no promises, as safety concerns or mandated reporting laws may require you to report the incident. Assure him or her that you will do everything in your power to prevent retaliation and stop further harassment. If you cannot answer their questions or address their concerns, assure the student you will connect them with someone who can.

DON'T DELAY.

If you cannot respond to the complaint, help the person connect with someone who can. If no one is available, assure the person you will find someone he or she can meet with as soon as possible. Then do it. Delays can make investigation difficult and can send a message to the person that the school is not taking the complaint seriously.

COMPLETE THE BULLYING/HARASSMENT REPORT.

Ask the person to write a summary of the incident.
Complete the Bullying/Harassment Report (Appendix E).
Ask the person how he or she would like the situation resolved and record the person's response.
Review the form you have completed with the person and make any corrections.
Ask the person to sign the form.

ENSURE THE PERSON'S SAFETY.

If the person feels safe returning to class, allow him or her to do so. If the person requests additional time or wishes to be excused to go home, accompany him or her to the main office. Assure the person you will be following up on the complaint and ask them to contact you regarding any continuing concerns.

FILE THE BULLYING/HARASSMENT REPORT.

Add any of your comments to the Bullying/Harassment Report, including observations of the person's demeanor.
Make copies of the report and the student's summary of the incident for yourself.
Submit copies of each to the student's counselor in a sealed envelope.
Submit the originals to the principal in a sealed envelope within 24 hours of receiving the complaint.

FOLLOW UP WITH THE STUDENT.

Contact the student the next day to ensure he or she is getting the needed assistance.

Response protocol adapted from that used by North High School, Eau Claire (Wisconsin) Area School District. Compiled by Deborah L. Tackmann and Life Promotions, Inc. Used with permission.

SAMPLE BULLYING/HARASSMENT REPORT

NOTE: WHENEVER POSSIBLE, HAVE THE STUDENT INVOLVED IN THE COMPLAINT COMPLETE THE TOP HALF OF THIS REPORT.

NAME OF STUDENT MAKING REPORT _____ DATE OF REPORT _____

DATE/TIME OF INCIDENT _____ LOCATION OF INCIDENT _____

NAME(S) OF INDIVIDUAL(S) SUSPECTED OF HARASSMENT OR BULLYING _____
_____

DESCRIPTION OF INCIDENT _____
_____

WITNESSES PRESENT _____

HOW WOULD THE STUDENT LIKE THIS RESOLVED? _____
_____

I hereby certify this is an accurate description of my written report. (Attach a copy of student's written report.)

_____   _____

SIGNATURE OF REPORTING STUDENT   DATE

NAME OF REPORTING STAFF MEMBER _____

COMMENTS _____
_____

☐ ADMINISTRATIVE INTERVENTION REQUESTED
☐ NO ADMINISTRATIVE INTERVENTION REQUESTED AT THIS TIME

ADMINISTRATIVE RESPONSE _____
_____

ORIGINAL Principal
COPIES Reporting staff member
       Counselor

Sample bullying report form adapted from that used by North High School, Eau Claire (Wisconsin) Area School District. Compiled by Deborah L. Tackmann and Life Promotions, Inc. Used with permission.

TEACHERS WANT TO CREATE AN INVITING AND HEALTHY ENVIRONMENT IN WHICH THEIR STUDENTS CAN LEARN, GROW AND BUILD STRONG RELATIONSHIPS. BUT STUDENTS COME FROM A VARIETY OF BACKGROUNDS AND OFTEN EXPERIENCE CIRCUMSTANCES AND SITUATIONS CAUSING THEM TO REACT IN WAYS THAT CAN HURT OTHERS BY ACTING OUT OR BULLYING. AS AN EDUCATOR, IT'S IMPORTANT TO RESPOND APPROPRIATELY.

1. GET CONNECTED. Consult with your principal or administrator to learn more about your school's policies and procedures regarding bullying. Collaborate with other teachers and leaders about your specific situation and develop a joint strategy.

2. OFFER A SAFE PLACE FOR THE VICTIM/TARGET. Do this in a way to offer him or her dignity and to feel safe from retaliation. Increase supervision to assure the bullying behavior is not repeated. Work with the child to develop a strategy of how best to respond if they are bullied again.

3. OFFER A SAFE PLACE FOR THE BULLY. Many bullying prevention programs suggest ways to hold the bully accountable, but fail to pursue the underlying issues spawning their negative behavior. Set up regular meetings with the student. Provide a safe place for him or her to confide about their life and why they are acting out. Show you care. If the only time a teacher or administrator meets with the child is to reprimand them, there is little opportunity to explore what's really going on in their lives and help them turn a corner.

4. ENCOURAGE BYSTANDERS TO BECOME "UPSTANDERS." Teach those who may witness bullying how they might intervene or get help by infusing lifeskills into your school's curriculum and staff development. Tell them you noticed their inaction or, conversely, if you were pleased with the way they tried to help. Create an environment where bullying behavior is knowingly unacceptable among peers, while fostering a culture of respect and dignity for everyone.

5. NOTIFY OTHERS. Let colleagues and parents of the student who is bullying know about their behavior. Let the student know they are being observed and what is expected of them. When speaking with parents or guardians, offer the Top 10 Bullying Prevention Tips for Parents (Appendix G), as well as other materials in this book, to help them respond appropriately.

6. STEP OUTSIDE THE CLASSROOM. Observe and engage with students outside the classroom. Building healthy relationships with students can create a more inviting atmosphere and can encourage students to talk openly and honestly with trusted adults about bullying.

7. TAKE ACTION. If you see bullying taking place, intervene immediately. It's okay to ask another adult to help. Talk to the kids involved separately, and don't make the kids involved apologize to patch relationships on the spot. To avoid escalating the tension, wait to sort out the facts and talk to the parties involved once they are calm.

8. BOOST CONFIDENCE. Encourage students to get involved in special activities, interests and hobbies to boost confidence, make friends and protect them from bullying behaviors. Having an outside focus can also provide an outlet for a potential bully to find value in something besides the feeling of power they experience when engaging in hurting others.

9. LIVE IT OUT. Students should know and understand the values you expect from them, and the values that your school and you personally uphold: respect, kindness, love and understanding. Live it. Model how to treat others with kindness and respect. Post these expectations in your classroom, staff lounge and school hallways.

10. CONDUCT BULLYING PREVENTION ACTIVITIES. Be an advocate in your school for activities, such as all-school assemblies, communications, activism, campaigns or creative arts contests, which highlight your school's values and reinforce that behaviors, such as harassment, bullying and/or other types of school abuse or violence, are not acceptable.

Tips compiled from U.S. Department of Education, *http://www.ed.gov/blog/2012/04/top-5-ways-educators-can-stop-bullies/* and U.S. Department of Health & Human Services, *http://www.Stopbullying.gov* by Deborah L. Tackmann.

APPENDIX G | FOR PARENTS: TOP 10 BULLYING PREVENTION TIPS

IT'S HEARTBREAKING TO LEARN THAT YOUR CHILD IS THE VICTIM OF BULLYING. SOMETIMES IT TAKES EVERYTHING IN YOU NOT TO REACT POORLY WHEN YOU KNOW YOUR CHILD IS BEING HURT, EITHER EMOTIONALLY OR PHYSICALLY. IF YOUR CHILD'S TEACHER INFORMED YOU, OR IF YOUR CHILD CONFIDED IN YOU, THAT HE OR SHE IS BEING BULLIED, OR SUSPECT THEY MAY BE A VICTIM, THERE ARE HEALTHY MEASURES YOU CAN TAKE.

1. TALK ABOUT IT. Talk about bullying with your kids and have other family members share their experiences. Ask your children about their day and listen to them talk about school, social events, their classmates, and any problems they have. If your child opens up about being bullied, praise him or her for being brave enough to discuss it and offer unconditional support.

2. STICK TOGETHER. Friends sticking together at school and elsewhere are less likely to be targeted than a child who is alone. Help your child learn how to avoid unsafe situations, and reassure them it's okay to talk to a teacher, counselor or adult in charge if they feel at risk or in danger.

3. DON'T FIGHT BACK. Don't encourage your child to fight. This could cause him or her to get hurt, get in trouble with the law, and initiate more serious problems with the bully. Teach kids to solve problems without using violence and praise them when they do.

4. TEACH AND LEARN LIFESKILLS. In Chapter 10, Part 3 of the book, *Dignity Revolution*, by Bob Lenz, students are given practical step-by-step applications on how to express their needs and respond to harassment, and are given examples of how to appropriately respond to a bully. Go through this chapter with your child and role-play to help them practice these skills.

5. KEEP CALM AND CARRY ON. If a bully strikes, a child's best defense may be to remain calm, ignore hurtful remarks, tell the bully to stop and simply walk away. Bullies thrive on hurting others. A child who isn't easily ruffled has a better chance of staying under a bully's radar.

6. DON'T TRY TO FIGHT THE BATTLE YOURSELF. Talk to your child's teacher instead of confronting the bully's parents. If the teacher doesn't act to stop the bullying, speak with the principal. Sometimes talking to a bully's parents can be constructive, but it's generally best to do so in a setting where a school official, such as a counselor, can mediate.

7. TAKE ACTION. If you see bullying taking place, step in and try to stop it, even if it is your own child doing the bullying. Don't treat bullying as a passing phase or something inevitable.

8. BOOST CONFIDENCE. Special activities, interests, and hobbies can boost confidence, help students make friends and protect them from bullying behavior. Involving them in activities outside of school and away from the negative environment created by a bully can help build strong relationships and an additional support network.

9. LIVE IT OUT. Make sure your children know and understand the values your family upholds: respect, kindness, grace, love and understanding. And live it. Model how to treat others with kindness and respect. If your children see you hit, ridicule or gossip, they are more likely to do so themselves, or have a poor self-image, making them more susceptible to being bullied. Help build empathy for others. Encourage your child to help others who need it and to be a friend.

10. BE SUPPORTIVE. Consult with the school to learn its policies and find out how staff and teachers can address the situation. Support and get involved in bullying prevention programs in your child's school. If your school doesn't have a program, consider starting one with other parents, teachers and concerned adults. Help build a culture of respect and dignity for every person.

Tips compiled by Deborah L. Tackmann.

PLACE YOUR NAME IN THE BLANKS BELOW.

_____ is patient, love is kind and is not jealous;
_____ does not brag and is not arrogant,
does not act unbecomingly; it does not seek its own, is not provoked,
does not take into account a wrong suffered,
does not rejoice in unrighteousness, but rejoices with the truth;
bears all things, believes all things, hopes all things,
endures all things.
_____ never fails;
But now faith, hope, love, abide these three;
but the greatest of these is love.

I Cor. 13:4-8, 13 *New American Standard Bible*. Used by permission.

CITATIONS

CHAPTER 2

1 Finn, Charles C. "Please Hear What I'm Not Saying," Sept. 1966. Used with permission. *http://www.poetrybycharlescfinn.com/pleasehear.html*

CHAPTER 4

1 American Society for Aesthetic Plastic Surgery (Mar. 12, 2013). "Cosmetic Procedures Increase in 2012" [news release]. Accessed *http://www.surgery.org/media/news-releases/cosmetic-procedures-increase-in-2012*

2 S. R. Dube, R. F. Anda, C. L. Whitfield, et al. "Long-term consequences of childhood sexual abuse by gender of victim." *American Journal of Preventive Medicine* 28 (2005): 430-438

3 S. L. Murphy, J.Q. Xu, and K. D. Kochanek, U. S. Department of Health and Human Services, Centers for Disease Control and Prevention, National Center for Health Statistics, National Vital Statistics System, National Vital Statistics Reports, "Deaths: Preliminary Data for 2010," Jan. 11, 2012, Vol. 60, No. 4.

4 U.S. Department of Health and Human Services, Centers for Disease Control and Prevention, Injury Center, "Violence Prevention." Web-based Injury Statistics Query and Reporting System (WISQARS), 2010. Accessed *http://www.cdc.gov/injury/wisqars/index.html*

5 Marketdata Enterprises, Inc. (2012). "U.S. Weight Loss Market Forecast To Hit $66 Billion in 2013" [market report]. Accessed *http://www.prweb.com/releases/2012/12/prweb10278281.htm*

6 U.S. Department of State, Bureau of Public Affairs, Fact Sheet, "The State Department and USAID Budget," Apr. 10, 2013. Accessed *http://www.state.gov/r/pa/pl/2013/207212.htm*.

CHAPTER 6

1 U.S. Congress, Martin Niemöller. *Congressional Record,* 1968, 90th Cong., 2nd sess., 114 (31636), Washington, D.C., U.S. Government Printing Office.

2 U.S. Department of Health and Human Services, Centers for Disease Control and Prevention, FastStats, "Suicide and Self-Inflicted Injury," 2013. Accessed *http://www.cdc.gov/nchs/fastats/suicide.htm*

3 *The 9/11 Commission Report: Final Report of the National Commission on Terrorist Attacks Upon the United States,* 2004, Washington, D.C., U.S. Government Printing Office. Accessed *http:// www.9-11commission.gov/report/911Report.pdf*

4 U.S. Executive Office of the President, Department of Defense, Office of Management and Budget, "The Federal Budget: Fiscal Year 2012." Accessed *http://www.whitehouse.gov/omb/factsheet_department_defense*

5 K. Rodham and K. Hawton. "Epidemiology and Phenomenology of Nonsuicidal Self-injury" in *Understanding Nonsuicidal Self-Injury: Origins, Assessment, and Treatment*, ed. Matthew K. Nock (Washington: APA® Books, 2009) 37-62

HISTORICAL RESOURCES

Henry L. Plaine, *Darwin, Marx, and Wagner: A Symposium* (Columbus, OH: Ohio State University Press, 1962)

Robert G. L. Waite, *The psychopathic god: Adolph Hitler* (New York: Basic Books, Perseus Books Group, 1977)

Sheree Owens Zalampas, *Adolf Hitler: A Psychological Interpretation of His Views on Architecture, Art and Music* (Madison, WI: Popular Press, imprint of University of Wisconsin Press, 1990)

CHAPTER 7

1 U.S. Department of Health and Human Services, Centers for Disease Control and Prevention, Office of Surveillance, Epidemiology, and Laboratory Services, Morbidity and Mortality Weekly Report, "Youth Risk Behavior Surveillance—United States, 2011," June 8, 2012, Vol. 61, No. 4. Accessed *http://www.cdc.gov/mmwr/pdf/ss/ss6104.pdf*

CHAPTER 8

1 Abraham H. Maslow. "Maslow's hierarchy of human needs," *Motivation and Personality*, 2nd ed. (New York: Harper & Row, 1970). Reprinted by permission of HarperCollins Publishers.

2 I Cor. 13:4-8, 13, *New American Standard Bible* (The Lockman Foundation, 1995). Used by permission.

CHAPTER 10 | PART 4

1 P. R. Smokowski and K. H. Kopasz. "Bullying in school: An overview of types, effects, family characteristics, and intervention strategies," *Children and Schools* 27 (2005) 101-109

2 Stop Bullying Now Foundation (Nov. 2013). "School Bullying affects us all" [report]. Accessed *http://www.stopbullyingnowfoundation.org/main/*

3 U.S. Department of Health and Human Services, Centers for Disease Control and Prevention, Office of Surveillance, Epidemiology, and Laboratory Services, Morbidity and Mortality Weekly Report, "Youth Risk Behavior Surveillance—United States, 2011," June 8, 2012, Vol. 61, No. 4. Accessed *http://www.cdc.gov/mmwr/pdf/ss/ss6104.pdf*

SOURCE

The lifeskills presented in this chapter have been created and/or used by Deborah L. Tackmann.

ABOUT THE AUTHORS

BOB LENZ

International Speaker and Author
Founder and President, Life Promotions

For more than 30 years, Bob Lenz has brought a message of value, courage and respect to more than three million people in all 50 states and throughout the world. His rare combination of passion, delivery and substance has resulted in Bob Lenz's school assembly programs consistently ranking among the best in the nation by school administrators, teachers, parents, and most importantly, students.

A storyteller at heart, Bob weaves humor together with heart-gripping illustrations to awaken students' understanding and inspire them to embrace their worth and impact their world with newfound purpose and resolve. He has studied at Teen Challenge, Riverside, California, and worked in cooperation with Students Against Destructive Decisions; Mothers Against Drunk Driving; BETA Clubs; National Association of Secondary School Principals; National Honor Society; National Association of Student Councils; Boys & Girls Clubs of America; Future Farmers of America; Family, Career and Community Leaders of America; and other notable organizations.

Bob's greatest joy remains his family, including wife Carol, five children and several grandchildren.

DEBORAH L. TACKMANN
B.S., M.E.P.D.

National Teachers Hall of Fame
National Health Educator of the Year Awards

Deborah Tackmann has over 30 years of experience as a health and physical education instructor. Tackmann received her bachelor of science degree from the University of South Dakota, and her master's degree from the University of Wisconsin-Eau Claire. She has been recognized by *USA TODAY* as one of the top teachers in the nation and is the recipient of national Health Educator of the Year awards from the American School Health Association and American Association for Health Education. An author, health consultant, coach, adjunct university faculty member and mother of three, Deb is an exceptional educator with a passion to inspire and empower others to be happy, healthy and successful in life. She has presented hundreds of cutting-edge seminars and keynotes in over 35 states.

Deb, who taught health education at North High School, Eau Claire, Wisconsin, presented at the 2012 National Conference on Bullying, sponsored by the School Safety Advocacy Council, where she received, on behalf of North High School, the National Exemplary Bullying Program and Individual Award. In June, 2012, Deb was the first teacher from Wisconsin to be inducted into the National Teachers Hall of Fame.

As an educator, she has dedicated her life to making a positive difference in the lives of children … one child at a time.

OTHER BOOKS BY BOB LENZ

Grace: For Those Who Think They Don't Measure Up
A faith-based exploration of the many facets of grace, and a call to live in freedom.

This is Life: Real Stories from the Road
Twenty-five true short stories from the travels of Bob Lenz, sharing joy and triumph, hurt and heartache, and most of all … hope

Available at *lifepromotions.com*

ENDORSEMENTS

I have known my friend, Bob, for a number of years and one thing that always stands out for me is that he really cares—I mean truly, genuinely and authentically really cares for people. With his typical engaging personality, *Dignity Revolution* will show you more about his heart and his mission to help individuals everywhere grasp their inherent dignity. Through Bob's words, I hope you will see your great worth and purpose.
AARON KAMPMAN | GREEN BAY PACKERS (2002-2009) PRO-BOWL (2006-2007)

If you asked me who could write a book on the subject of bullying, I would say you have discovered the best person to do it. Bob Lenz is someone who radiates love for others through his everyday life. I struggled to fight through the darkness resulting from my personal experience with bullying. As a result, I made multiple attempts to take my life. Bob's words shined a light and gave me hope. I am now here to share my story and help empower others. May this book also shine a light into your life so you and many others can impact this world in amazing ways.
AMY BURG | STUDENT

Bob has humanized the issue of bullying in a way that will help each of us quickly recognize that we have a personal responsibility to stamp out bullying in our homes, schools and society.
JASON E. LEAHY | EXECUTIVE DIRECTOR, ILLINOIS PRINCIPALS ASSOCIATION

Bob Lenz has an incredibly valuable message for young people. He's gifted in delivering it through both the written and spoken word. The message in *Dignity Revolution* is one of his most important, told in a very readable and touching way. This is a book that parents should read with their children and talk about.
DICK BENNETT | HIGH SCHOOL AND COLLEGE BASKETBALL COACH

With wit, passion and a clear understanding of the world of youth and their bare grief, Bob Lenz has hit it out of the park with this one. Every few paragraphs are enough for a whole youth discussion on bullying. Buy this. Use this. Grow from it. Grow beyond it. Don't let this one go.
RICH MELHEIM | CEO, FAITH INKUBATORS

Over 30 years ago, a young, enthusiastic teenager, Bob Lenz, came to my door selling pizza for what would be the beginning of a worldwide movement. We've forged a friendship since then, and it's been my privilege to support his amazing organization. Bob humbly uses humor, passion and life experiences to reach the broken-hearted and shamed.
DONNA JOHNSON | EXECUTIVE NATIONAL VICE PRESIDENT, ARBONNE INTERNATIONAL, LLC

As an adolescent psychiatrist, I'm routinely asked to help teenagers cope with mental and emotional suffering, and as a discerning clinician, it's clear to me that the scourge of bullying will not succumb to scientific treatment alone. *Dignity Revolution* provides a clear, accessible roadmap toward such a solution. This book should be required reading for all youth, and for anyone who interacts with young people. Beyond this, I wholeheartedly recommend *Dignity Revolution* to anyone who has ever bullied another person, or been bullied. I believe that should cover all of us.
KENNETH C. CASIMIR, M.D. | PEDIATRIC/ADOLESCENT PSYCHIATRIST, AFFINITY BEHAVIORAL HEALTH

STANDING UP FO
VALUE OF EVER